COPELAND MARKS'
Indian & Chinese Cooking
From the Himalayan Rim

ALSO BY COPELAND MARKS

False Tongues and Sunday Bread: A Guatemalan and Mayan Cookbook

Sephardic Cooking

The Great Book of Couscous

COPELAND MARKS'
Indian & Chinese Cooking
From the Himalayan Rim

M. Evans and Company, Inc.
New York

First published by Donald I. Fine Books, an imprint of
Penguin Books USA Inc.

Trade paperback edition published by
M. Evans and Company, Inc.
216 East 49th Street
New York, New York 10017

Map by Dick Garland

Illustrations from the Brooklyn Botanic Garden's hand-
book *Oriental Herbs and Vegetables*, 1983, reprinted
with the permission of Stephen K-M. Tim and the
Brooklyn Botanic Garden.

Designed by Irving Perkins Associates

ISBN 0-87131-885-7
CIP data is available

Printed in the United States of America

9 8 7 6 5 4 3 2 1

⊰ ACKNOWLEDGMENTS ⊱

WRITING A cookbook of ethnic cuisines from faraway places is a study in appropriation. The writer must (or should) travel and appropriate recipes and folklore from someone somewhere.

There are those who give willingly, others who urge you on with encouragement, and those who withhold or refuse to release culinary information through lack of historical perspective. I have met them all.

In a cookbook of this sort many gave because they understood the importance of recording old family recipes before they disappeared into the twentieth century. And, there were those whose assistance was important or indispensable. For example, Suresh and Sheila Kumar of Calcutta were unstinting in their help. Rishi Kumar gave me important leads to unknown sources. Victoria Jahn of the Brooklyn Botanical Garden Library, like a detective, found botanical information that I required. Then there were the following:

For the Hakka Chinese
   Jennifer Chen
   Michelle Chen
   Johnny Chen (chef)
   Mama Chen
   Paul Hsiung
   Chung Chiu Yun Hsiung

For the Marwaris
   Saroj Nowlakha
   Anju Chopra Dugar
   Shakuntala Dadha
   M. Mahipal Dadha

For the Jewish Way with Pickles and Chutneys
   Helen Nahoum
   Norman (Nahoum) Nahoum

For the Armenians
  Basil Aratoon
  Rosie David
  Sahag and Sirarti Kalaydjian, Gulbenkian Library, Old City
    Jerusalem

For the Bengal Club—English Colonial, Calcutta
  Prabhat Kumar Datta, Food and Beverage Consultant, Advisor of
    the Bengal Club. He is the colonial employee *par excellence*, a
    sturdy, intelligent man with fifty years service.

For Bhutan
  Jigme Tenzing and his wife, Phuntsho Wangmo
  Nima Dorji
  Princess Namden Dorji

For Sikkim
  Phuchung Lepcha

For Frontier Cooking of Kashmir
  Panna Lal Sharma

For Mizoram
  Chazan Gideon Rei
  Mafaka Lalfakzuala and his wife, Maawmi

☩ GLOSSARY ☩

Ajowan — Sometimes called *yamani* (*Trachyspermum copticum* or *ammi*), this is a member of the umbellifer family and is related to caraway, fennel, dill, cumin, coriander, and parsley. This is a highly regarded small, erect plant with enormous medicinal properties. The seeds are widely used in India to treat many ailments, such as colic pains, delirium, migraine, flatulence, as well as for drunkenness and as a poultice for insect bites. Thymol, an antiseptic, is the oil from *ajowan* seeds.

    The use of *ajowan* in food, leaving its slight medicinal flavor, may have started as a panacea for illnesses and was gradually incorporated into the cooking rather than the other way around.

Amchoor (dry mango powder) — This is the pulp of acid green mango that is first sliced off the large central seed, dried in the sun, then ground into a powder. It is a popular seasoning among the Marwaris.

Chayote (Sechium edule) — I first discovered this excellent pear-shaped vegetable in Guatemala and liked it immediately for its flavor, ease of cooking, and the variations of types—from a pale beige to dark charcoal green. The vines were tied in family gardens on upright frames, with the chayote hanging down like giant grapes.

    I was surprised to find that this essentially Central American vegetable was growing in wild profusion on the hillsides surrounding Gangtok, the capital of Sikkim. It was called "sqoosh" (squash) by the people there and had been integrated into the cuisine. The chayote in Sikkim are large, pale green, and weigh about one pound each.

Chinese Okra (Luffa acutangula) — Also called ridge gourd, this is not okra at all. The characteristic long, curved shape, with parallel ridges, is visible all over Asian markets. The Hakka Chinese use this gourd in stir fries. You must slice off the ridges before cooking.

Elephant Trunk Chili — is about 3 to 4 inches long, curved and twisted and, in fact, looks like an elephant's trunk. This is the name that was described to me in India. The chili is semi-hot and has a clean taste and is always used fresh. It can be either green or red.

Fennel (Foeniculum vulgare) — The seeds are frequently used in Kashmiri food. They have an aromatic aroma and flavor resembling anise and are considered to stimulate the appetite and assist digestion, among other attributes. Like all the spices used in India, there is both a culinary and medical equation.

Fenugreek (Trigonella foenum-graecum) — A popular spice in India, fenugreek is slightly bitter when used alone, but is often included in curry powders. It has considerable mucilage, becoming sticky when used in one of the Jewish table chutneys of Calcutta. It is especially popular in Kashmiri food and has many medicinal properties, such as the ability to lower one's blood pressure and assist digestion.

Garam Masala—a traditional mixture of spices (such as curry powder) which differs from region to region and family to family. It frequently includes cardamon, coriander (Chinese parsley), cumin, black pepper and cinnamon.

Gundruk — This vegetable is the dried *saag* (spinach-like greens) that is collected and dried for the winter season. Large quantities are first put into a pit in the ground, pressed for days, then removed, with most of the moisture evaporated. Then it is air-dried and packaged for easy handling. In the winter, it is reconstituted with water and stir fried, as it could be when eaten fresh.

Hing (Ferula asafoetida) — I have heard it described as obnoxious (phew!) and expletive deleted! It is a powerful seasoning of the carrot family that is used in very small quantities to give a preparation more dimension. In this respect it is eminently successful. It is popular in Bengal and among the Marwaris.

Nettle (Urtica dioica L.) — The nettle, a perennial weed that is grown all over Sikkim, is filled with vitamins and minerals. The Sikkimese prepare a fine soup, slightly viscous, from the young leaves. It is known to regulate digestion and promote the function of the liver and kidneys. Trust the native for his knowledge of herbs and spices and for the ability to live off the land.

Tree Ears (Auriculoria polytricha) — Sometimes known as cloud ears, these are a very popular dried fungus eaten in Sikkim.

They expand at least three times their dried size when soaked in water.

Water Chestnuts (also pani phal) (Trapa natans) — I used to have my cook buy these juicy snacks during the monsoon season in Calcutta when they would make their appearance in the markets and at the street vendors. The chestnuts look like the dark head of a water buffalo with two curved horns. A white nut was inside. They are eaten fresh, although sometimes they are cooked (see Vegetarian Cooking of the Marwaris, page 36).

⚔ CONTENTS ⚕

⚛ INTRODUCTION ⚛

CALCUTTA IS my culinary universe in India. A strange choice, you might say, but a very effective one for me. I had worked in Calcutta for five years and have always felt comfortable there. My friendships have been useful and the generally pleasant and cooperative attitude of the people of this vibrant, teeming, horrendous city has made it possible for me to research several books and articles on Indian food.

However, I can never forget how Rudyard Kipling wrote about Calcutta with these words:

> *Where the cholera, the cyclone, and the crow*
> *come and go;*

As true today, with some modifications, as it was then.

Ethnic foods, the only kinds that interest me, are a result of shared history and similar group identification. This also includes religion and race, especially religion, since it can and often does influence the choice of foods (kosher for Jews and halal for Muslims). The four "outsider" communities that follow are good examples of this.

The people of Calcutta are divided into two groups, which I have designated. There are the insiders and the outsiders. The *outsiders* are to me more interesting from a culinary point of view. They are the Baghdadi Jews, the Parsis, the Armenians, and the Hakka Chinese, people who have lived in Calcutta in established communities for centuries. They have developed their own cuisine and were never homogenized into the racially Indian caste system, but continued to live within the framework of their religious and cultural pasts. Their food is conspicuous by its differences from the standard recipes and eating habits of the Indians. It is wonderful!

The *insiders* are the Bengalis, the people of the state of Bengal, who are the original inhabitants, with their own cultural agenda. I have written about them in my book, *The Varied Kitchens of India*.

From Calcutta at the center, I traveled on and off for many years to the Himalayan regions of Kashmir, Sikkim, Nepal, Darjeeling, getting around with ease and always returning to Calcutta. It is this personal odyssey from a culinary point of view that I have recorded in this book.

Calcutta is a microcosm of the various kitchens found in India, each one drawing from the spices and seasonings available, incorporating them into their cuisine, producing a unique and valuable addition to the styles of cooking in this great subcontinent.

PART ONE

THE COOKING OF CALCUTTA:

Ethnic Diversity and Flair

⚔ 1 ⚔

THE COOKING

OF THE HAKKA CHINESE

SEVERAL ACCOUNTS document the origin of the Hakka Chinese community in Calcutta. These accounts were gleaned from the Hakka themselves rather than being published in scholarly works. The Hakka constitute a relatively young immigration into Calcutta, unlike the Parsis, Jews, and Armenians who have lived there for centuries.

One account states that the first Hakka was Achu, who came from southeast China, in the region of Canton, and settled in the town he established now known as Achipur. The Hakka were alleged to be a nomadic group of people that plied the rivers in their boats and could move from one town to another. There is a group of Hakka, for instance, in Malaysia who differ in a culinary way from those I discovered in Calcutta.

Achipur, the name taken from Achu, is thirty kilometers over a perilously rough road from Calcutta. Reputed to have occurred prior to the Moghul Empire in the sixteenth century, now all that remains on the tranquil banks of the Hooghly River, a tributary of the Ganges, as it flows its muddy way past Calcutta to the Bay of Bengal is an unprepossessing ashram in the town of Achipur to tell us that Achu was there.

About a half mile further down the river on a winding, narrow dirt road is his tomb, which faces the river. It is nothing more than a maroon-painted clay semicircle in the Chinese fashion. When I visited the tomb, several villagers suddenly appeared with their black goās to point out the tomb of the saint known as Achu Sahib. During February and March the Hakkas of Tangra and Calcutta make a pilgrimage to the ashram and tomb of Achu.

Another account of the establishment of the Hakka community

indicates that the bulk of the Hakka came to Calcutta from southeast China about one hundred years ago and developed a thriving business based on leather tanning. It is arguably logical, since the Hindus would not traffic in the skins of the sacred cow, that the Buddhist Hakka would.

At the height there were about thirty thousand people in the Hakka enclave known as Tangra. After the Sino-Indian conflict of 1962, the community dwindled to about ten thousand. Like the other outsiders in India, the Parsis, Jews, and Armenians, the Hakka have emigrated to other countries.

In the meantime, Tangra, which is a tangled conglomeration of unpaved streets, narrow alleys, houses, and tanning factories, is also the center for small, simple Chinese restaurants, so popular with the Calcutta crowd. In spite of Tangra's obvious lack of modern amenities, it was always a pleasure for me to take a taxi to Tangra, about thirty minutes from the center of Calcutta, to have a meal, take cooking lessons, and spend time with these enormously charming and likable people—the Hakka of Calcutta—with their own style of ethnic cooking.

ZA HA YA
Shrimp Ball Appetizer

1 pound peeled shrimp (1 1/4 pounds with shells, then peeled)
1 inch fresh ginger, peeled and chopped fine
1 tablespoon light soy sauce
1/8 teaspoon salt
1/8 teaspoon pepper
1/4 teaspoon chopped hot green chili
* 3 tablespoons flour*
* 2 tablespoons cornstarch*
* 1 whole egg*
*   Oil for deep-frying*

1. Put all the ingredients, except the oil, in a food processor and grind to a not-too-smooth mixture. (Some texture is required.)
2. Heat the oil in a wok or skillet over moderate heat. Drop rounded tablespoonfuls of the shrimp mixture into the hot oil and brown on all sides, about 2 minutes. Drain on paper towels. Serve warm or at room temperature.

Makes about 22 shrimp balls.

TSA KYOW
Fried Wontons with
Potato and Cashew Stuffing

1 *pound potatoes, boiled in their jackets, peeled, and mashed*
2 *tablespoons chopped roasted cashew nuts*
2 *sprigs fresh coriander (Chinese parsley), chopped fine*
1 *teaspoon salt*
1/8 *teaspoon pepper*
30 *wonton skins, 3 inches square*
2 *cups peanut oil for deep-frying*

1. To prepare the stuffing, mix together well the mashed potatoes, cashews, coriander, salt, and pepper.
2. Take 1 wonton skin, place a heaping teaspoon of the stuffing almost in the middle of it, and fold in the style known as "nurse's cap." Or, fold according to the more modern shortcut method. See Note below. Prepare 30 wontons and set aside.
3. Heat the oil in a wok over moderate heat until hot. Drop in a few wontons at a time, stirring gently and turning them until brown and crisp. Remove and drain on paper towels. Fry the remaining wontons in the same manner. Serve warm or at room temperature.

Makes 30 wontons.

VARIATION
PRAWN AND PORK STUFFING

1/2 *pound ground pork*
1/4 *pound prawns, peeled, deveined, and chopped*
1 *teaspoon cornstarch*
1 *teaspoon salt*
1/8 *teaspoon pepper*

Mix all the ingredients together well. Stuff and fry the wontons as directed above.

Enough stuffing for 30 wontons.

NOTE: There are several ways of folding wonton skins. Nowadays, a young lady sits in the window of the modern meat markets in New York's Chinatown, folding wontons in the modern method, which, she will tell you, is easier and faster than the old-fashioned method known as the "nurse's cap," named for its resemblance to the pointed hat.

Nurse's Cap—Wonton skins (wrappers), about 3 inches square, can be purchased in Chinese supermarkets. Place 1 teaspoon of the filling, vegetarian or meat, slightly off-center in the middle of a wrapper. Fold the wrapper in half, pressing it together gently. Now fold it over once more. Take the corner edges of the bottom fold and pull them toward each other, pressing one over the other. (This is not difficult to do as the wrapper skin is thin and flexible. A dab of water and a little pressure will seal the wonton into a rounded nurse's cap shape.

Modern Method—Place 1 teaspoon of the filling in the middle of the wrapper. Fold the opposite corners together to shape a triangle.

Take the top of the triangle and fold it over just enough to meet the other side. Now take the end of the twice-folded wrapper and pinch it like an accordian toward the other end.

Grasp the top end and fold it over to meet the bottom pinched end. A dab of water will seal the 2 ends together. This wonton will be about 3/4 inches wide at the top and 1 1/2 inches long, with a pointed bottom.

Dumpling Style—There is an ingenious plastic machine that folds a *round* wonton wrapper into a crinkle-edged dumpling. The machine is a small rectangular press, which allows you to fold it over and seal the dumpling. Place a round wonton skin in the machine, place 1 teaspoon of the filling in the center, moisten one rounded side of the skin with oil, and fold the machine over firmly to seal the dumpling into a half moon. The crinkled edge is produced by the design of the plastic.

The dumplings can be cooked in boiling water for 5 minutes or deep-fried until brown.

K A N G
Hakka Soup

Chinese okra is not okra at all, but of the vegetable sponge family, *Luffa acutangula*. It is a long, slender gourd-like vegetable with ridges that run along its length. The ridges should be trimmed off before using.

1 cup dried mushrooms
1 tablespoon peanut oil
1/2 pound ground pork
2 quarts chicken stock
1 Chinese okra (see Glossary), ridges removed and discarded and cut into
    1/2-inch cubes (2 cups)
1/2 teaspoon salt
1/4 teaspoon pepper
2 tablespoons cornstarch dissolved in 1/4 cup cold water
1 egg, beaten
3 scallions, sliced thin for garnish

1. Soak the mushrooms in water for 10 minutes. Drain and slice.
2. Put the oil in a wok over moderate heat, add the pork, and stir-fry it for 3 minutes. Add the chicken stock and bring to a boil.
3. Add the mushrooms, okra, salt, and pepper and simmer for 1 minute. Pour in enough of the cornstarch mixture to just thicken the soup. Cook, stirring for 1 minute.
4. Dribble in the egg, stirring slowly for 1 minute. Garnish with the scallions. Serve hot.

Serves 8–10.

TIE SOON
Mixed Seafood Soup

This Hakka soup has a rich assortment of ingredients in a lightly thick-ened chicken stock base to which a touch of lemon juice has been added.

2 *quarts homemade chicken stock*
8 *dried black mushrooms, soaked in water 10 minutes, drained, and sliced*
1/4 *cup small shrimp, peeled and chopped*
1/2 *cup fresh crabmeat*
2 *tablespoons fresh lemon juice*
2 *tablespoons light soy sauce*
1/4 *teaspoon salt*
2 *tablespoons cornstarch dissolved in 1/4 cup cold water*
1/4 *cup fresh coriander (Chinese parsley) leaves*

1. Put all the ingredients, except the cornstarch mixture and co-riander, into a large pan. Bring to a boil, then simmer over moderate heat for 10 minutes.
2. Stir in the cornstarch mixture slowly, adding only enough to thicken the soup lightly to the desired thickness. Stir in the coriander. Serve hot, especially in winter.

Serves 8.

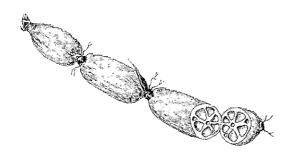

N S T U T O N G
Shark Fin Soup

One day my Hakka cooking teacher brought out from her well-stocked kitchen a large plastic bag filled with the translucent fibres of shark fins knotted together in a tangled mass. Ten grams of this costly and presti-gious food were weighed out for the soup, soaked in water for 1/2 hour to separate the fibres, then drained. The rest is history.

  5 *cups water*
  1 *teaspoon salt*
1/8 *teaspoon pepper*
  1 *teaspoon peanut oil*
1/2 *teaspoon MSG (optional, but a strong Hakka recommendation)*
 10 *grams shark fin fibres, soaked in water 1/2 hour and drained*
1/2 *cup chopped boneless chicken*
3/4 *cup fresh crabmeat*
  1 *tablespoon cornstarch dissolved in 3 tablespoons cold water*
  6 *fresh coriander (Chinese parsley) leaves for garnish*

1. In a pan bring the water, salt, pepper, oil, and MSG if used, to a boil over moderate heat for 1 minute.
2. Add the shark fin fibres, chicken, and crabmeat, and bring to a boil. Add the cornstarch mixture in a thin stream, stirring constantly, for 3 minutes until the soup is thickened. Garnish with the coriander leaves. Serve hot, in Chinese soup bowls.

Serves 10.

NOTE I do not recommend MSG at any time as fresh vegetables and other ingredients have their own message. The Hakkas I knew heartily en-joyed the use of this taste-enhancer, however.

TSOY SOON
Buddhist Vegetable Soup

This soup was served to me and others at a Buddhist temple during a joyful prayer gathering as one of their vegetarian preparations.

  4 cups water
  1 package (1/2 ounce) cellophane noodles, soaked in cold water 15 minutes and drained
  5 dried black mushrooms, soaked in water 10 minutes, drained, and sliced
  1 square Chinese tofu (bean curd), cut into 1/2-inch cubes
  1 can baby corn, drained and cut into 1/2-inch pieces
1/4 cup grated carrot, for color
1/2 cup button mushrooms, sliced
  1 teaspoon vegetable oil
  1 teaspoon salt
1/8 teaspoon pepper
  1 teaspoon cornstarch dissolved in 2 tablespoons cold water
 10 fresh coriander (Chinese parsley) leaves

In a large pan bring the water to a boil over moderate heat. Add all the ingredients, except the coriander, and boil for 2 minutes. Add the coriander. Serve hot, in Chinese soup bowls.

Serves 10.

AAP PE POLOPETSU
Duck Soup with Daikon

1 *young duck (about 2 pounds) or 1/2 large duck*
2 *quarts water*
2 *pounds* daikon *(Oriental white radish), peeled and cut into 2-inch-thick round pieces*
2 *teaspoons salt, or to taste*
1/8 *teaspoon pepper*
10 *fresh coriander (Chinese parsley) sprigs*

1. Cut the duck into 16 pieces. Put them in a pressure cooker with the water. Cover and pressure cook for 15 minutes. Open the cover, add the *daikon*, salt, and pepper, and cook without the pressure over moderate heat for 15 minutes.
2. Trim off the stem ends of the coriander sprigs and cut the herb into 1-inch pieces. When ready to serve the soup, add the coriander. (Adding it in advance blackens the leaves, which is not desired.) Serve hot.

Serves 8.

STOW KOO
STUMEE HONG
Straw Mushroom and Corn Soup

2 *quarts chicken stock*
1 *cup canned straw mushrooms*
1 *cup fresh corn kernels or canned, drained*
1 *teaspoon salt*
1/8 *teaspoon pepper*
2 *teaspoons cornstarch dissolved in 3 tablespoons water*
1 *whole egg, beaten*

1. Put the chicken stock in a large pan and bring to a boil. Add
   the mushrooms and corn and simmer over moderate heat for 5
   minutes. Add the salt and pepper.
2. Add just enough of the cornstarch mixture to the soup to
   thicken it lightly. Simmer for 2 minutes. Dribble in the egg, in
   a steady stream, stirring slowly, for 1 minute. Serve hot.

Serves 8.

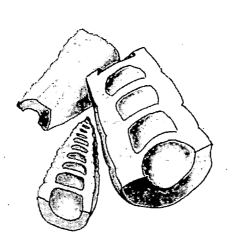

SUI MIEN
Egg Noodle, Chicken, and Seafood Soup

1 tablespoon cornstarch
1/4 cup each boneless chicken, cut into 1/2-inch cubes; any sea fish, cut into
    1/2-inch cubes; small shrimp, peeled; or thin pork, cut into julienne strips
1 pound fresh egg noodles
2 tablespoons peanut oil
2 quarts homemade chicken stock
1/2 cup thinly sliced cabbage
1 large carrot, sliced into julienne strips (1 1/2 cups)
1/2 pound Chinese okra (see Glossary), ridges removed and sliced thin
2 teaspoons salt, or to taste
1/4 teaspoon pepper
3 scallions, sliced thin

1. Mix the cornstarch with the meat and fish of choice. (The combination may be an assortment of all the suggestions or limited to 2 or 3.) Set aside.
2. Soak the noodles in *boiling* water for 5 minutes. Drain in a colander, then mix with the peanut oil.
3. Bring the chicken stock to a boil over moderate heat in a large pan. Add the meats, seafood, noodles, vegetables, salt, and pepper and cook rapidly for 3 minutes. Remove from the heat and stir in the scallions. Serve hot.

Serves 8.

STOW MIEN
Fried Noodles with Assorted Vegetables

A light vegetarian combination with noodles to serve no matter the season.

1 pound fresh egg noodles
5 tablespoons peanut oil
2 scallions, cut into 2-inch pieces
1 small carrot, cut into julienne slices (1/2 cup)
1 medium onion, sliced thin (1/2 cup)
3/4 cup bean sprouts, the tails pinched off
3 tablespoons light soy sauce
1/2 teaspoon pepper, or more if you prefer a peppery taste

1. Cook the noodles in boiling water for 5 minutes. Drain in a colander, then mix with 2 tablespoons of the oil to prevent the noodles from sticking together. Set aside.
2. Heat the remaining 3 tablespoons oil in a wok over moderate heat and add all the vegetables. Stir-fry for 2 minutes. Add the noodles, soy sauce, and pepper and stir-fry for 5 minutes. Serve warm.

Serves 6.

PA STAM KE
Steamed Chicken

The Hakka are partial to farm-raised chicken that feed on natural foods and it's what's recommended for this simple dish, one of their most popular and best examples of home-cooking.

1 whole young chicken (3 pounds with some fat)
1 tablespoon salt

1. Rinse the chicken well in cold water. Drain. Rub the salt over and inside the chicken and let stand overnight in the refrigerator.
2. Place the chicken in a Pyrex bowl and steam, covered, in a Chinese-style steamer over moderate heat for 40 minutes. A small amount of broth will accumulate
3. Disjoint the chicken and cut it into 12 pieces. Pour the broth over all. Serve with white rice.

Serves 8.

NOTE: This is a useful recipe as the chicken can also be served cold or boned and incorporated into a salad.

TSOON KE
Deep-fried Spring Chicken

Everyone in the family—men, boys, and girls—learned to cook from their enthusiastic mother in the kitchen. Observing, tasting, smelling, and remembering the aromas all contributed to an encyclopedic knowledge of the Hakka style of cooking. It is the Hakka family way.

1 *spring chicken or Cornish game hen (2 pounds), cut into 16 pieces, or the equivalent in boneless chicken parts*
2 *inches fresh ginger, peeled and ground to a paste*
6 *cloves garlic, peeled and ground to a paste*
1 *egg, beaten*
1 *teaspoon soy sauce*
1/2 *teaspoon salt*
4 *tablespoons cornstarch*
Oil for deep frying

1. Mix the chicken, ginger, garlic, egg, soy sauce, salt, and 2 tablespoons of the cornstarch together well. Set aside for 10 minutes. Dredge each piece of chicken lightly in the remaining cornstarch.
2. Heat the oil in a wok over moderate heat and drop in the chicken, one piece at a time. Fry until brown crisp for about 5 minutes. Drain on paper towels. Serve warm as an appetizer with drinks or in a meal.

Serves 8.

HSUAN TSANG BUDDHIST TEMPLE

I was invited to attend the celebration of the Lady God at the Hsuan Tsang Buddhist Temple in the 24 Parganas district on the far outskirts of central Calcutta. My taxi took me from Tangra, the leather center controlled by the Hakka Chinese, on a convoluted journey through small isolated Indian villages, past open fields, meandering narrow rivers, and lush tropical landscape. We arrived in the middle of nowhere.

The extended and colorful temple consisted of several prayer halls built in 1973 with a two-story barracks-like complex for visiting pilgrims.

The celebration was attended principally by women, with only a handful of men, myself, a Hakka friend and male family members from the environs of Tangra. Prayers were officiated by the head monk, the Reverend Wu Chien, in the principal hall where one wall was covered by the large and colorful statues of the Lady Buddha and her attendants. There was a constant chattering by the women and the prayers were chanted in an atmosphere of informality rather than awe.

Then came the Buddhist vegetarian lunch. The large spacious kitchen was hot, the blazing gas burner was needed according to the cook, my friend's mother, for stir-frying enough dishes for the eighty people who were attending. The cook was good, really good, and unflappable in the heat pouring out of the stove. Subsequently, I took cooking lessons from this admirable woman at her home.

This was the menu of the day, no meat, poultry or fish.

Tsoy Soon
(Buddhist Vegetable Soup)
Tsoy Ten
(Mushroom, Cauliflower, and Cashew Stir Fry)
Tao Mientin
(Gluten, Bean Sprout, and Preserved Carrot Stir Fry)
Stow Mien
(Fried Noodles with Assorted Vegetables)
Munlo Pet
(Chinese White Radish in Black Bean Sauce)
Toufu
(Bean Curd with Tomato and Black Mushrooms)
Tsa Kyow
(Fried Wontons with Potato and Cashew Stuffing)
Tang Kow
(Hakka Sponge Cake)

STA KYO KE
Hakka Fried Chicken

Draining the fried chicken in a strainer removes most of the oil so that the pieces are crispy without being greasy.

1 1/2 pounds Cornish hens, cut into 12 pieces
2 tablespoons flour
2 tablespoons cornstarch
3/4 teaspoon salt
1/8 teaspoon pepper
2 teaspoons light soy sauce
1 inch fresh ginger, peeled and chopped fine
1 teaspoon hot green chili, chopped fine
1/2 cup oil for frying

1. Mix the chicken well with the flour, cornstarch, salt, pepper, soy sauce, ginger, and chili. Let stand 1/2 hour. This is an important step in establishing the flavor.
2. Heat the oil until hot in a wok over moderate heat. Add the poultry and fry for 10 to 15 minutes, which is enough time to brown the pieces. Remove with a slotted spoon and drain in a metal strainer for 1 or 2 minutes. Serve warm.

Serves 8.

MON FAN

Rice with Chicken, Mushrooms, and Chinese Sausage

This wonderful dish is also called *hakka biryani* as it vaguely resembles the Muslim dish, which is prepared with lamb. The Spanish have their paella.

When the cool season, November, begins, the Hakka ladies begin to prepare their sausage, tying two of them together with thick string and hanging them on a clothesline to dry in the cool air.

The two types of dried mushrooms used in cooking are the black type common in China, Korea, and Japan. They are imported and expensive. The other type is the wild mushroom dried in the hill station of Shillong, Assam, the famous tea region. These are soft and smaller than black mushrooms but have an earthy flavor that reflects their wild origins. I have both kinds and use both.

1 pound boneless chicken, cut into slender slices, 2 inch by 1/2 inch wide
1 cup whole dried mushrooms, rinsed well, soaked in warm water for 10 minutes, and drained
1 teaspoon light soy sauce
1 tablespoon cornstarch
2 tablespoons peanut oil
6 dried Chinese sausage, cut on the diagonal 1/4 inch wide
3 pounds rice (6 cups), rinsed well, soaked in water for 1/2 hour, and drained
6 cups water
1 teaspoon salt

1. Combine the chicken with the mushrooms, soy sauce, and cornstarch, tossing well to coat.
2. Heat the oil in a wok or large pan and stir-fry the sausage over moderate heat for 1 minute. Add the chicken and mushroom mixture and continue to stir-fry for another minute.
3. Add the rice, water, and salt and bring to a boil. Stir a moment

to mix, cover the pan, and cook the mixture over the lowest heat until the rice has absorbed the water and the rice is soft. This will take about 15 minutes. Stir everything together to integrate the flavors. Serve warm.

Serves 10.

The Hakka Buddhist Temple, Hakka Chinese

TSE STOY STOW KE KUE
Mixed Vegetables with Chicken

3 *tablespoons peanut oil*
1/2 *pound boneless chicken, cut into 3/4-inch cubes*
1 *head garlic (8 cloves), chopped*
1 *sweet green pepper, cut into 1-inch cubes (1 cup)*
1 *small carrot, cut into julienne strips (1/2 cup)*
1 *medium onion, quartered and separated into pieces (1 cup)*
1/4 *cup Chinese okra (see Glossary), sliced into diagonal pieces*
1/4 *cup cubed bok choy, white part only*
1/4 *cup cauliflower florets*
1 *cup chicken stock*
1 *teaspoon salt*
1/8 *teaspoon pepper*
1 *tablespoon light soy sauce*
2 *tablespoons cornstarch dissolved in 4 tablespoons cold water*
Coriander (Chinese parsley) leaves for garnish

1. Heat the oil in a wok over moderate heat. Add the chicken and stir-fry for 2 minutes until the color changes. Add the garlic and stir-fry until golden; do not let darken.
2. Add the green pepper, carrot, onion, okra, bok choy, and cauliflower and stir-fry for 3 minutes, mixing everything together well. Do not overcook the vegetables to avoid a loss of vitamins.
3. Add the chicken stock and cook, stirring, for 5 minutes, adding the salt, pepper, and soy sauce. Stir in the cornstarch mixture, a little at a time, adding just enough to add texture but not so much that the mixture is gummy. Garnish with coriander leaves. Serve warm with rice.

Serves 8.

NOTE: The Hakka recommend chopped garlic for its curative properties, especially when it comes to stomach upset. Chop 2 or 3 cloves garlic, put them in a spoon, then swallow them quickly, chewing as you go along. This garlic fix, especially among the Hakka, is popular and effective.

K E K O N
Chicken Liver Stir Fry

Those who like chicken livers—and I am one of them—will appreciate this resourceful recipe (there are not that many of them). My Hakka friend saved livers from every chicken killed in her kitchen, which guaranteed a fresh supply at all times.

2 *tablespoons peanut oil*
1 *pound chicken livers, divided into lobes*
1 *medium onion, sliced thin (1/2 cup)*
1 *sweet green pepper, cut into 1-inch cubes (1 cup)*
1 *small hot green chili, sliced thin*
2 *tablespoons water*
1 *tablespoon soy sauce*
1 *teaspoon salt*
1/2 *teaspoon sugar*
1/8 *teaspoon pepper*

1. Heat the oil in a wok, add the chicken livers, and stir-fry over moderate heat for 1 minute. Add the onion and green pepper and stir-fry for 3 minutes. Add the chili.
2. Mix together the water, soy sauce, salt, sugar, and pepper and add to the wok. Stir to combine well and stir-fry 2 minutes more. Serve warm.

Serves 4 or 5.

L O O A A P
Roast Duck in a Wok

> The ducks in Hakka Tangra are small so that one can find a duck that is actually two pounds when cleaned. Elsewhere, however, ducks are four or five pounds in which case 1/2 will be enough to prepare this recipe.

 1 *2-pound young duck or 1/2 of a large duck*
 1 *cup peanut oil*
 3 *ounces garlic, peeled and cracked*
 5 *whole dried red chilis*
 3 *inch cinnamon stick*
10 *whole star anise*
 2 *tablespoons dark soy sauce*
 2 *tablespoons oyster sauce*
 2 *tablespoons sugar*
1/8 *teaspoon salt*
1/8 *teaspoon pepper*
 1 *cup water or chicken stock*

1. Steam the duck in a Chinese-style steamer over hot water at moderate heat for 15 minutes . Remove and cool the duck.
2. Put the oil in a wok and over moderate heat add the garlic, chilis, cinnamon, and star anise and stir-fry for 2 or 3 minutes, or until the garlic turns golden in color. Add the duck and fry it on all sides for 5 minutes.
3. Add the soy sauce, oyster sauce, sugar, salt, and pepper. Cook for another 5 minutes and add the water or stock. Reduce the heat to low, cover the wok, and simmer for 20 minutes. If the duck is still too firm cook until tender, 10 minutes more. Remove the duck, cut it into 8 serving pieces, and pour the small amount of sauce that remains over the pieces. Serve warm.

Serves 8.

LAPSANG FATOSY
Cauliflower and Chinese Sausage

  1 tablespoon peanut oil
  6 dried Chinese sausage, cut on the diagonal into 2-inch-long slices
3/4 cup water
  2 pounds cauliflower, cut into 1-inch florets
1/2 teaspoon salt
1/2 teaspoon sugar
  1 teaspoon soy sauce
· 1 teaspoon cornstarch dissolved in 1 tablespoon water
  1 sprig fresh coriander (Chinese parsley) leaves, chopped, for garnish

1. Heat the oil in a wok, add the sausage and 1 tablespoon water, and stir-fry over moderate heat for 2 minutes.
2. Add the cauliflower, salt, sugar, and soy sauce and stir-fry for 1 minute. Add the remaining water and cook until it has nearly evaporated. Then add the cornstarch mixture to thicken the sauce to taste. Some sauce will remain at the end of the cooking time. Garnish with the coriander. Serve warm.

Serves 8.

FOONG MOON STUNYO
Garlic Pork in Rice Wine

  2 *pounds pork belly, with 3 layers of meat and fat cut into 1-inch pieces*
  4 *tablespoons vegetable oil*
 30 *cloves garlic, peeled and cracked*
1/4 *teaspoon salt*
  1 *tablespoon soy sauce*
  2 *tablespoons rice wine*
  1 *teaspoon sugar*
  1 *tablespoon oyster sauce*
  2 *cakes bean curd or 1 cup dried black mushrooms, soaked in water 10*
    minutes and drained
  1 *cup water*

1. Blanch the pork belly in boiling water for 1 minute. Drain.
2. Put the oil in a wok and stir-fry the pork over moderate heat
   for 10 minutes. Add the garlic, salt, soy sauce, rice wine, sugar,
   oyster sauce, bean curd or mushrooms, and water. Bring to a
   boil, then transfer the mixture to a pressure cooker and cook
   for 15 minutes; or cook in the wok over low heat for 1 hour.
   Some sauce will remain at the end of the cooking time.

Serves 8–10 with rice and other dishes.

NOTE: I was amazed to learn that the Hakka in their enclave in Tangra
   were avid users of pressure cookers because they save time as well as
   fuel. Gas is the most common type of cooking energy. I have found that
   the pressure is very effective in some cooking instances and relish the
   idea of a return to this most useful pot.

SON KYAM HSA
Sweet-and-Sour Prawns

Prawns are large shrimp, but you see the word used generically for any kind of shrimp in Calcutta. This is a classic dish, especially popular in Hakka restaurants.

1 *pound prawns, shelled but with tails intact*
1 *tablespoon cornstarch*
1 *tablespoon flour*
1/8 *teaspoon salt*
1/8 *teaspoon pepper*
1 *whole egg*
1 *tablespoon soy sauce*
  Oil for deep-frying
1 *small cucumber, halved lengthwise, seeds removed, and cut into 1/2-inch pieces*
1 *sweet green pepper, cut into 1/2-inch cubes (1 cup)*
1 *small tomato, cut into 1-inch cubes (1/2 cup)*
1 *small carrot, sliced thin on the diagonal (1/2 cup)*
1 *medium onion, quartered and separated into pieces (1 cup)*
1/4 *cup tomato ketchup or tomato sauce*
4 *cloves garlic, chopped fine*
1 *teaspoon sugar*
1 *tablespoon lemon juice*
1/2 *cup water*
1 *teaspoon cornstarch dissolved in 2 tablespoons water*
1 *scallion, sliced thin, for garnish*

1. Mix together the prawns, cornstarch, flour, salt, pepper, egg, and soy sauce.
2. Heat the oil until hot in a wok and fry the prawn mixture over moderate heat for 2 minutes or until the color changes to golden. Remove the prawns from the oil and drain briefly on paper towels.
3. Remove all the oil from the wok except 2 tablespoons. Add the cucumber, green pepper, tomato, carrot, onion, and tomato

ketchup and stir-fry over moderate heat for 2 minutes. Add the garlic and stir-fry 1 minute more.

4. Add the sugar, lemon juice, water, and cornstarch mixture and cook for 2 minutes. Add the prawns and mix well. Garnish with the scallion. Serve hot.

Serves 8.

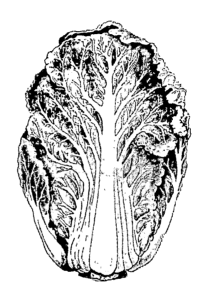

CHE ZSE NN
Steamed Pomfret

Here is a classic method of steaming fish that fulfills all our modern requirements for healthy cooking.

2 *pounds whole saltwater fish, such as pomfret, red snapper, porgy, or another of choice*
3 *tablespoons peanut oil*
1 *large onion, sliced (1 cup)*
1 *inch fresh ginger, peeled and sliced into julienne strips*
3 *tablespoons soy sauce*
1/8 *teaspoon pepper*

1. Clean the whole fish, remove the gills, and rinse well in cold water. Score the fish on the diagonal twice on each side. Place the fish on a platter that will fit into a Chinese-style steamer.
2. Put the oil in a wok over moderate heat, add the onion, ginger, soy sauce, and pepper and stir-fry for 2 minutes, or until the onion becomes golden in color. Pour the hot oil over the fish.
3. Steam the fish, covered, in the steamer over moderate heat for 1/2 hour. Serve warm.

Serves 8–10.

HAKKA CHOW
Fried Noodles Hakka Style

Various Calcutta eating places serve *Hakka chow* but in an Indianized style, which means adding other seasonings and sometimes vegetables. Here is the real thing, which I prefer.

1/4 cup peanut oil
1/2 pound boneless chicken, cut into slender 2-inch pieces
 1 teaspoon cornstarch
1/2 pound small prawns (shrimp), peeled and deveined but left whole
 1 small carrot, cut into julienne strips (1/3 cup)
 1 cup thinly sliced cabbage
 2 small onions, sliced (1/2 cup)
 2 pounds half-cooked fresh egg noodles, cut in half
 1 teaspoon salt
1/8 teaspoon pepper
 2 tablespoons soy sauce
 4 scallions, sliced thin

1. Heat the oil in a wok. Mix the chicken and cornstarch together, add it to the oil, and stir-fry over moderate heat for 2 minutes. Add the prawns and stir-fry another minute. Add the carrot, cabbage, and onions and continue to stir-fry for 2 minutes.
2. Add the noodles, reduce the heat to low, and add the salt, pepper, and soy sauce. Stir well, sprinkle with the scallions, and toss again. Serve warm.

Serves 8.

T O U F U
Bean Curd with
Tomato and Black Mushrooms

The Hakka Buddhists do not use onion, garlic, or spring onions (scallions). Seasoning and flavorings are achieved by ingredients naturally combining with each other.

2 cups dried black mushrooms
1 tablespoon peanut oil
1 large tomato, sliced (1 1/2 cups)
10 squares Chinese tofu (bean curd), coarsely crushed (do not purée)
1 cup water
3 tablespoons light soy sauce
1 teaspoon salt, or to taste
1 teaspoon sugar

1. Soak the mushrooms in water for 10 minutes. Drain and slice.
2. Heat the oil in a wok or large skillet over moderate heat, add the tomato, and stir-fry it for 2 minutes. Add the mushrooms and stir-fry for 2 minutes more.
3. Add the tofu and continue to stir-fry for 2 minutes more. Add the water, soy sauce, salt, and sugar and bring to a boil. Cook for 1 minute. (The mixture will be thin.) Serve warm with rice.

Serves 10.

NOTE: Some cooks prefer to thicken this dish. Should you wish to do so, mix 2 teaspoons cornstarch with 2 tablespoons water. Add this to the cooking mixture, stirring it in after the water has boiled and simmering it for 2 minutes.

NYONG TAO KON
Stuffed Bean Curd

The snakeskin fish called for below is unique in that to my knowledge it is not available in New York. In fact, the skin is tough and snakelike, but it is the flesh that we are concerned with, and it is smooth and so viscous it can be pulled off the bones with your fingers and easily mashed. The Hakka prefer this fish as it combines well with the pork. A possible substitute would be the soft flesh of whiting or well puréed fillet of sole.

1/2 *pound ground pork*
  6 *medium dried black mushrooms, soaked in water 10 minutes, drained, and chopped*
1/2 *pound snakeskin fish, mashed with fingers*
  1 *teaspoon salt, or to taste*
1/2 *teaspoon pepper*
  3 *tablespoons cornstarch*
  3 *squares Chinese tofu (bean curd), cut into 4 triangles each*
    Oil for deep-frying

1. Prepare the stuffing: Mix together well the pork, mushrooms, fish, salt, pepper, and cornstarch. Set aside.
2. Cut a 1-inch-long slash into the side of each bean curd triangle near the top. Do not cut all the way through.
3. Into the slit carefully push in 1 heaping tablespoon of the stuffing. Then press extra stuffing over the flap and the top of the triangle. (What one sees is a rounded ball over the top of the triangle.)
4. Heat the oil in a wok over moderate heat. Add the stuffed triangles, one at a time, and deep-fry until brown on all sides. This will take about 5 minutes. Remove from the oil and drain briefly on paper towels. Served warm with a soy sauce dip. Or, serve in individual bowls of hot chicken broth. I prefer this method.

Serves 4 to 6.

MUNLO PET
Chinese White Radish in Black Bean Sauce

This dish was one of the ones offered for lunch at the Buddhist Temple.
Of course, it is vegetarian.

1/4 cup peanut oil
1 inch fresh ginger, peeled and smashed with the flat side of a cleaver
1 3/4 pounds Oriental white radish (daikon), peeled and cut into 1-inch-
wide round slices
1 teaspoon sugar
1 teaspoon salted black beans
2 1/2 cups water
1 tablespoon cornstarch dissolved in 3 tablespoons water
10 leaves fresh flat-leaf parsley for garnish

1. Heat the oil in a wok or pan. Add the ginger and stir-fry over
moderate heat for 30 seconds. Add the radish, sugar, and black
beans and stir-fry for 1 minute.
2. Add the water and cook over moderate heat until the radish is
soft, about 10 to 15 minutes. Add just enough of the cornstarch mixture in a slow stream to thicken the sauce, stirring
continuously, and cook for 2 minutes. There will be substantial
sauce. Garnish with the parsley. Serve warm.

Serves 10.

TSOY TEN
Mushroom, Cauliflower, and Cashew Stir Fry

> Mushrooms and cashew nuts give this stir fry substance, texture, and a meatiness that is one of the hallmarks of Buddhist vegetarian cooking.

3 tablespoons peanut oil
2 small carrots, cut into 1/4-inch dice (1 cup)
1 sweet green pepper, cut into 1/2-inch cubes (1 cup)
1 pound cauliflower, cut into 1-inch florets
1/2 pound fresh mushrooms, halved
1/2 teaspoon salt
1/2 teaspoon sugar
1 tablespoon light soy sauce
1/2 cup water
1/4 cup whole cashew nuts, roasted

1. Heat the oil in a wok over moderate heat, add the carrots, and stir-fry for 1 minute. Add the green pepper and cauliflower, and stir-fry another minute. Add the mushrooms and stir-fry for 1 minute more.
2. Add the salt, sugar, soy sauce, water, and lastly the cashew nuts. Stir-fry for 2 more minutes to integrate all the flavors. Serve warm with rice.

Serves 10.

NOTE: Until recent years, India was the largest producer in the world of cashew nuts. This probably explains why the Hakka use these rich oily nuts—they are so easily available. The nuts fulfill their culinary destiny in this vegetarian dish.

TĀNG KOW
Hakka Sponge Cake

This delightful cake was served at the Buddhist Temple one joyous morning. Only egg whites are used here, which is acceptable to the Buddhists, who are vegetarian. The smallest drop of yellow food coloring will produce a colored cake. The coloring is purely optional. The Hakkas, in fact, like the color. Without it, the cake is white. Either way the taste is unchanged.

12 *egg whites, at room temperature*
 8 *tablespoons sifted flour*
10 *tablespoons sugar*
 3 *tablespoons butter, melted*
   Drop of yellow food coloring (optional)

1. Beat the egg whites with a whisk until stiff. Add the flour, 1 tablespoon at a time, folding it in until it is no longer visible, then adding another measure until all the flour is used.
2. Add the sugar all at once and mix it in briskly. Last, pour in the melted butter and food coloring, if used, and mix well.
3. Line an 8- or 9-inch round or square cake pan, 3 inches deep, with wax paper and pour in the batter.
4. Bake in a preheated 350 degree oven for 20 to 25 minutes, or until a wooden skewer comes out clean. The cake will rise. Remove and cool before serving.

Serves 10.

⫷ 2 ⫸
VEGETARIAN COOKING
OF THE MARWARIS

THE MARWARIS are the preeminent business community in India with remarkable mercantile genius. Their business acumen is famous and ubiquitous. They are Hindus with a closely knit joint family system. Their caste is of the Vaishias or merchants.

What is not so well known is that they are also the most conservative of vegetarians, with a variety of foods that is idiosyncratic and a broad inclusion of spices and seasonings that are sometimes mindboggling.

Jain Marwari Temple, Calcutta

Jain Marwari Festival Procession, Calcutta

The home of the Marwaris (the people from Marwar) is (or was) in the state of Rajasthan in northwest India. It is an arid wasteland, not suitable for much except raising camels. Millet *(Pennisetum typhoideum)* and sorghum *(Sorghum vulgare)* are two drought-resistant crops that can be grown in the region and are utilized by the Marwaris. Perhaps this is one of the reasons why there was an explosion of emigration from Rajasthan in the eighteenth and nineteenth centuries to cities like Calcutta, where they established a tradition of trading, which was all the more surprising since their homeland was an arid semi-desert. They prospered, assisted by their strong attachment to family and caste.

The Marwaris equate food and medicine and are constantly conscious of the efficacy of certain foods that produce good health. To this day, vegetarianism has its exponents that are principally concerned with health and the prevention of illness.

A perusal of the recipes that follow will illustrate that there is a pronounced use of many spices and seasonings that heighten the flavor of essentially simple grains and vegetables. How else to prepare, for example, coarsely ground millet (see Rabari, page 46), except with the use of cumin laced wth slightly acid yoghurt? Another extraordinary example (see Mardiea, page 49) uses over ten different spices and seasonings in not insignificant amounts in a complex interchange of spice paste with grain broths and chick-peas. The Marwari use of spices is inspired and geared to making something out of nothing.

Ancient Indian history is filled with references to the use of spices. Turmeric, with its golden color, is much liked. Asafoetida (*hing*), with its admittedly off-putting odor, is used in minute quantities as a flavor *enhancer*. Marwari cooking has an analytical approach to the use of spices and what effect they can produce in the foods being cooked at the moment.

There are several subdivisions among the Marwaris. I cooked with families that belonged to the Agarwalla group and the Jains. It is safe to say that all Jains, for example, are Marwaris, but not all Marwaris are Jains. It is sometimes a division of ideas from one class of Marwari to another. We know that the Jains have an enormous respect for animals and in previous generations wore a mouth mask so as not to injure insects.

The common thread for all Marwaris is their devotion to commerce and vegetarianism, both of which have reached a high degree of eminence and respectability.

DHANIA CHUTNEY
Fresh Coriander Chutney

What would an Indian table be without one of the numerous side dishes of condiments—read chutneys—that one expects when dining? Here are two popular types that grace the Marwari table.

  3 *ounces fresh coriander (Chinese parsley) leaves, tough stems removed*
2–3 *fresh hot green chilis, sliced*
1/2 *teaspoon cuminseed*
1/4 *teaspoon salt*
1/8 *teaspoon* hing *(asafoetida; see Glossary)*
1/2 *teaspoon water*
  1 *tablespoon lemon juice*

In a food processor grind all the ingredients to a paste. Serve with any kind of Indian food. Refrigerate for up to 2 days.

Makes about 1/2 cup.

DHANIA PUDEENA KA CHUTNEY
Fresh Coriander and Mint Chutney

This chutney is best served the same day it is made.

3 ounces fresh coriander (Chinese parsley), tough stems removed
1 ounce fresh mint leaves
1/2 teaspoon cuminseed
1 teaspoon water
1/4 teaspoon salt
1/8 teaspoon hing (asafoetida; see Glossary)
1 tablespoon lemon juice

In a food processor grind all the ingredients to a paste. Serve with any kind of Indian food.

Makes about 1 cup.

L E H S U N C H U T N E Y
Garlic Chutney

There was a time when the ultra conservative Marwari Jains would not eat onion, garlic, ginger, or even spring onions (scallions). Times change and there is a relaxation in dietary rules, except for the religious commitment to vegetarianism, which never changes. This chutney is a nicely spiced table condiment to be tasted with Marwari foods or any other Indian foods.

    1 *tablespoon dried garlic powder (see Note)*
1/2 *teaspoon salt*
1/2 *teaspoon red chili powder*
    1 *tablespoon ground coriander*
1/2 *teaspoon* amchoor *(dried ground mango; see Glossary)*
    2 *tablespoons water*
    2 *tablespoons vegetable oil*
1/2 *teaspoon cuminseed*
1/4 *teaspoon turmeric*
1/2 *teaspoon paprika*

1. Make a smooth paste with the garlic powder, salt, chili powder, coriander, *amchoor,* and water.
2. Heat the oil in a wok or skillet over a medium/low heat. Add the cuminseeds, which will float in a matter of seconds. Then add the turmeric, paprika, and the garlic paste. Stir rapidly for 1 minute. If too thick, add another tablespoon water, stirring it in quickly. Remove from the heat; the chutney is ready. Serve at room temperature.

Makes about 1/4 cup.

NOTE: To make dry garlic, dry 10 large cloves garlic, peeled, in the hot sun as it is done in the Rajasthan desert for 5 or 6 days. The desiccated garlic cloves are then ground to a brownish powder.

    One can also dry them in a very low oven overnight or, as I have done, left them on the central heating radiator during the winter season—any port in a storm. Process into a powder and store in a jar with a tight cover.

LАHSUN KА
CHUTNEY
Fried Garlic Chutney

For this remarkable chutney paste, the garlic is cooked so that it does not leave an unpleasant aftertaste. The mixture is enhanced considerably by the combination of spices. *Hing*, a potent, some would say offensive spice, is inevitably added, in a minute quantity, which does not clash with anything else. It must be included according to Marwari tastes.

THE GARLIC PASTE

1/2 cup cloves garlic, peeled and sliced
2 tablespoons water
1/4 teaspoon hot red chili powder
1/2 teaspoon salt
1/4 teaspoon ground coriander

THE BAGHAR

1 tablespoon ghee *(clarified butter) or butter, melted*
1/8 teaspoon hing *(asafoetida; see Glossary)*
1/4 teaspoon cuminseed
1/4 teaspoon black mustard seed

1. Prepare the garlic paste: Grind the garlic to a smooth paste with the water. Briskly stir in the chili powder, salt, and coriander. Set aside.
2. Prepare the *baghar:* Heat the *ghee* in a small skillet. Add all the spices and let them sizzle over low heat for 10 seconds.
3. Add the garlic paste and stir-fry for 2 minutes, which will color the chutney a light tan. Store in a jar with a tight cover in the refrigerator.

Makes about 1/2 cup.

N I M K I
Crispy Spice Snack

This is a very tasty cracker type snack that is served at teatime or any time. Often taken on journeys and picnics, these should be stored in a jar with a tight cover to retain crispness.

2 cups flour
1 teaspoon salt
1/2 teaspoon ground ajowan (see Glossary)
1/2 teaspoon black cuminseed (kala jeera, available in Indian markets)
1 tablespoon ghee (clarified butter)
2–3 tablespoons warm water
Oil for deep-frying

1. Mix everything together, except the water and oil. Then add enough of the water to make a firm dough. Cover the dough ball with a damp cloth and let it rest for 1/2 hour.
2. Cut the dough ball in half. Roll out 1 piece into a circle not more than 1/4 inch thick. Cut it into 2-inch diamond-shaped pieces.
3. Heat the oil in a wok over moderate/low heat, add a few dough pieces at a time, and fry until golden, a minute or two. Remove and drain on paper towels. Continue to fry the remaining dough pieces and drain them in the same manner.
4. Let cool and store in a jar with a tight cover. Serve at snack time with tea or coffee.

Makes at least 12 pieces.

C H U N N A
Whole Wheat Berries in Thick Milk

Chunna is a specialty of Phalodi village in Rajasthan. My Jain host, whose hobby was cooking his ancestral foods, prepared it for me with considerable confidence since it requires a number of steps and time.

Formerly *chunna* was garnished with real silver or gold leaf purchased, depending upon the wealth of the family, from the Hindu temple. When I questioned whether it was digestible, my host explained that many vegetables, such as spinach, contained iron and modest quantities of other minerals. So why not silver?

1 cup whole wheat berries (available at health-food stores)
4 cups water
7 cups milk
3/4 cup sugar
1/2 teaspoon ground cardamom
15 threads saffron
   Silver leaf for garnish

1. Sprinkle 1 teaspoon water over the wheat berries and pound them lightly in a stone or metal mortar with a pestle to remove the outer husks. Repeat the pounding again and discard the husks. (The whitish berries produce a whiter dessert.)
2. Cook the wheat berries in the water in a pressure cooker (a popular kitchen utensil in Calcutta) for 15 minutes; or for 1/2 hour in a regular saucepan.
3. Add the milk to the wheat berries and cook over low heat, stirring frequently to prevent the milk from burning, for 1/2 hour. The mixture will thicken.
4. Add the sugar, cardamom, and saffron and continue to cook until the milk sauce has thickened but is still fluid, about 15 minutes. (*Chunna* should have the consistency of oatmeal porridge.) Serve warm garnished with the silver leaf.

Serves 8.

NOTE: Wheat berries with the husks can also be used in this porridge. The color of the finished dish will be light beige instead of white, with a slight change in flavor that I was unable to detect. The Marwaris, however, know the difference.

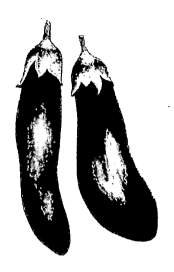

R A B A R I
Ground Millet Gruel

Rabari, like so many Marwari dishes, is a gruel that sometimes includes a milk product—in this case, yoghurt. An added touch is the slight fermentation, which is so indicative of the inventive nature of the Marwari—just letting nature take its course.

1 cup yoghurt

2 tablespoons coarsely ground millet (bajari ka daliya, available in Indian markets)

1 teaspoon salt

1/2 cup water

1/2 teaspoon ground cumin for garnish

Mix everything together except the cumin. Put the mixture in a pan and simmer over low heat, stirring so that the yoghurt does not separate, for 10 minutes. (The thin gruel will thicken somewhat.) Set aside, covered, at room temperature until the next day during which time it will develop a lightly fermented flavor. Serve cold with yoghurt and garnish with the ground cumin.

Serves 2 or 3 as a light dish for the hot summer days of Rajasthan.

PHULGOBI KA AKRA
Cauliflower Stir Fry

Cauliflower is the ubiquitous vegetable that seems to be included in every Marwari vegetarian dish I've ever tasted. It has the advantage of being a firm vegetable that retains its shape if not overcooked, yet it requires very little cooking, as this recipe demonstrates.

1/2 pound cauliflower
2 tablespoons peanut oil
1/4 teaspoon cuminseed
1/4 teaspoon turmeric
1/2 teaspoon salt, or to taste

1. Cut the cauliflower into 1-inch florets of equal size. Drop them into boiling water and cook over high heat for 2 minutes. Drain well and cool.
2. Heat the oil in a wok or skillet. Add the cauliflower, cuminseed, and turmeric and stir-fry over moderate heat for 2 minutes to lightly brown. Add the salt and stir to combine. Serve warm or at room temperature with rice, *puri* (made from whole wheat flour), or a fried *luchi* (prepared with white flour).

Serves 4.

VARIATION
PHULGOBI, ALOO, TOMATAR KA TERKARI
Cauliflower, Potato, and Tomato Stir Fry

1 recipe Cauliflower Stir Fry (above)
1/2 pound potatoes boiled in their skins, peeled, and cut into 1/2-inch cubes
1 tomato (about 1/4 pound), cut into 6 slices
1/4 teaspoon hot red chili powder
1/2 cup water
1 tablespoon chopped fresh coriander (Chinese parsley)

When the cauliflower has turned light brown as noted in the above recipe, add the potatoes and stir-fry 1 minute over moderate heat. Add the tomato, chili powder, and water and cook for 3 minutes. Sprinkle the coriander over all. Serve warm or at room temperature.

Serves 6 or more.

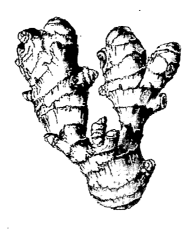

MARDIEA
Chick-peas in an Especially Spiced Sauce

Bagbar is the technique of quickly browning an assortment of spices in hot *ghee* or oil. The *ghee* is often heated in a large metal spoon over a flame and the spices are dropped in to sizzle for 10 seconds or so. Then it is dropped into the dish being prepared, such as Kidgeree or Mardiea, and immediately covered so that none of the aroma is lost.

    Mardiea is a highly inventive, heavily spiced preparation that only the Marwaris could have produced in India to satisfy their perfect vision of vegetarianism. The recipe is from the Marwari Murshidabad community, where more is frequently not enough.

THE DAL
To make *dal* water, use 1/2 cup yellow split peas (*channa*) and 4 cups water. Bring to a boil, and cook until the peas are soft. Let the mixture settle for 15 minutes, strain into a bowl, and reserve 2 cups of the liquid.

THE WHOLE WHEAT WATER
Dissolve 1 1/2 tablespoons whole wheat flour in 3 tablespoons water. Set aside

THE RICE WATER
To make rice water, cook 1 cup rice in 4 cups water for 10 minutes. Strain into a bowl and reserve 3 cups rice water.

THE SPICE PASTE
  1/4 teaspoon peppercorn
1 1/2 teaspoons cuminseed
  10 whole almonds
   4 cardamom pods, pod covers removed and discarded
   4 whole cloves
 1/2 inch fresh ginger, peeled and sliced
   2 tablespoons water

Grind all the ingredients together. Set aside.

THE *BAGHAR*
    2 *tablespoons* ghee *or butter, melted*
    4 *whole cloves*
    4 *whole cardamom pods*
    1/2 *teaspoon* cuminseed
    2 *bay leaves* (tej putta)
    1/8 *teaspoon* hing *(asafoetida, see Glossary)*
    1/2 *teaspoon hot red chili powder*
    1/2 *teaspoon* garam masala
    1/4 *teaspoon ground cinnamon*

Heat the *ghee* in a small skillet over low heat and add all the spices. Stir-fry for 10 seconds and add to the Mardiea liquid mixture. Bring to a boil and remove from the heat.

THE *MARDIEA*
    1 *tablespoon ground dried mango powder* (amchoor, *see Glossary); or 1 tablespoon lemon juice; or 2 tablespoons tamarind paste dissolved in 2 tablespoons water and strained*
    1 *teaspoon salt, or to taste*
    2 *cups cooked chick-peas*

Put the *dal*, whole wheat, and rice waters in a pan with the spice paste, mango powder (or other suggestions), salt, and cooked chick-peas. Bring to a boil over moderate heat. Add the freshly sizzled *baghar* and remove from the heat. Serve warm or room temperature with Kidgeree or plain rice.

Serves 6 or more with other dishes.

BESAN KA CHILLA
Chick-pea Flour Pancakes

These delectable Marwari pancakes are unsweetened and filled with an assortment of spices in Indian fashion. Garnished with onion, fresh coriander, and if desired thin slices of fresh green chili to taste, they make a nice snack.

1 cup besan (chick-pea flour)
1 teaspoon salt
1 teaspoon hot red chili powder
1/2 teaspoon ajowan seed (see Glossary)
1/16 teaspoon hing (asafoetida; see Glossary)
1/2 teaspoon coriander seed, crushed
1 teaspoon vegetable oil, plus additional oil for the skillet
1/2 cup water, or more as needed
1/2 cup chopped onion
1 tablespoon chopped fresh coriander (Chinese parsley)

1. Mix together into a smooth, thin batter (like a typical pancake batter) the besan, salt, chili powder, ajowan, hing, coriander seed, vegetable oil, and water. Stir the mixture well. If it is too thick, add 2 or 3 tablespoons water until it has batter consistency. Let rest 1/2 hour.
2. Heat a skillet with 1 teaspoon oil and rub it over the surface with a kitchen towel. Add 1 teaspoon water and 1/4 cup batter. Spread the batter out with the back of a spoon to a pancake 5 inches in diameter. Sprinkle with 1 teaspoon each of onion and coriander.
3. Fry the pancake over moderate/low heat for 2 minutes, turn it over, and brown the second side for 1 minute. The pancake will be soft and aromatic. Make pancakes with the remaining batter in the same manner. Serve warm at snack time with tomato ketchup (a popular modern touch).

Makes 8–10 pancakes.

GATTA
Vegetarian Sausages in Spiced Yoghurt Sauce

Marwari foods are often labor intensive and can involve several steps that gradually build up to a final impact. There is usually a servant or family member to cut, chop, and mix the sometimes intricate steps. Vegetarian dishes can be like this as ultimately they must provide a substitute for meat, poultry, and fish.

I was invited into the kitchen of Saroj, the beautiful wife in a several-story Marwari home. It was an honor and a rare occurrence for a foreigner to observe the how and why of her cooking and I was impressed.

Each step in the preparation of the sausages and sauce requires an additional amount of spices and seasoning but is offset somewhat by the yoghurt in the sauce. Vivid and textured, this is served as one of several dishes in a Marwari meal.

THE SAUSAGES
1 cup besan (chick-pea flour)
1/4 teaspoon hot red chili powder
1/2 teaspoon salt
2 teaspoons peanut oil, plus additional for frying
1/4 teaspoon ground coriander
1/4 teaspoon cuminseed
2 cups water

THE SPICED YOGHURT
1/4 teaspoon turmeric
1/2 teaspoon hot red chili powder
1 tablespoon ground coriander
1/4 teaspoon salt
1 cup yoghurt

THE BAGHAR AND SAUCE
2 tablespoons peanut oil
1/4 teaspoon cuminseed
1 bay leaf
1/8 teaspoon hing (asafoetida; see Glossary)

1 clove garlic, very thinly sliced
1 small fresh hot red chili
1 cup water

1. Make the sausages: Mix the *besan*, chili powder, salt, oil, coriander, cuminseed, and 2 or 3 tablespoons water into a firm dough. Divide it into 5 equal pieces, and shape each into a cigar 1/2 inch in diameter.
2. Put the balance of the water in a pan, bring to a boil, and add the sausages. Cook over moderate heat for 10 minutes. (They will float.) Remove the sausages and cut into 1/2-inch pieces.
3. Heat the oil in a skillet and brown the slices all over for about 3 minutes. Remove from the pan and set aside.
4. Make the spiced yoghurt: Mix the turmeric, chili powder, coriander, and salt together with 2 tablespoons of the yoghurt. Combine this paste with the remaining yoghurt and set aside.
5. Prepare the *baghar*: Heat the oil in a pan, add the spices, and stir-fry for 10 seconds. Add the spiced yoghurt mixture and stir-fry over low heat for 2 minutes.
6. Then add the water and bring to a boil. Add the sausages and cook over moderate heat for 5 minutes to thicken the sauce. Serve warm.

Serves 5 or 6 with other dishes.

GATTA KIDGEREE
Vegetarian Sausages and Rice

This is a most compatible combination, and a simple extension of the Gatta recipe.

1 cup rice, cooked and cooled
1 recipe Gatta (Vegetarian Sausages, page 52)

In a pan, heat the rice and sausages together over low heat for 5 minutes. Serve warm.

Serves 4.

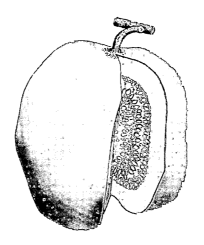

KHEERA CHANNA
DAL TERKARI
Cucumber and Lentil Mix

A true vegetarian dish, according to the Marwaris, must have fresh flavor (the cucumber) and protein (the yellow split lentils), plus sufficient spices and seasonings to make meat unnecessary. This mix fills the bill.

4 *young cucumbers (1 pound), peeled*
2 *tablespoons yellow split lentils* (channa ka dal)
1 *cup water*
1 *tablespoon peanut oil*
1/4 *teaspoon cuminseed*
1/8 *teaspoon* hing *(asafoetida; see Glossary)*
1/4 *teaspoon turmeric*
1/4 *teaspoon hot red chili powder*
1/2 *teaspoon salt*

1. Quarter the cucumbers lengthwise. Cut each quarter into 1-inch pieces.
2. Cook the lentils in the water over moderate heat for 5 minutes. Drain.
3. Prepare the *baghar:* Heat the oil in a wok or skillet, add the cuminseed and *hing*, and stir-fry over moderate heat for 10 seconds, until lightly brown. Add the cucumber and lentils and stir-fry for 1 minute. Add the turmeric, chili powder, and salt and cook, stirring continuously, over low heat for 5 minutes to soften the lentils. Serve warm.

    (There is no need to add water to this dish as the cucumbers release moisture and the lentils, which have been partially cooked, are moist.)

Serves 4.

KHEERA SIMLA MEERCHA KA TERKARI
Cucumber and Capsicum Mix

The green pepper sold in American supermarkets is a *capsicum*, the word used in England, India, and some other Asian countries for this same vegetable. In this case, it is linked with Simla, a famous hill station established during the British colonial period so that the colonials in New Delhi could escape the heat. The *capsicum* grows well in the cool mountain air and is much in demand. Here you substitute green peas for the yellow split lentils in the recipe above.

1 large sweet green pepper, seeded and cut into 1/2-inch cubes (2 cups)
2 tablespoons fresh green peas

Add the cucumber, pepper, and peas all at once to the oil; then add the spices, using the same cooking method above. Serve warm.

Serves 4.

R A H R I
Cucumber Salad in Mustard Sauce

Mustard seed is a popular spice in the state of Bengal, where Calcutta is situated. In the absence of mustard seed, one can use dried mustard powder, which has almost the same power as the seeds, but be prepared to adjust the amount.

2 cups cubed peeled Kirby cucumbers (1/4-inch cubes)
1 or 2 teaspoons black mustard seed, to taste, ground to a paste with 1 tablespoon water
1/2 teaspoon salt
1 tablespoon lemon juice, or more to taste
1 teaspoon finely chopped fresh hot green chili

Mix all the ingredients together. Taste and adjust the salt and lemon juice if necessary. Serve cold or at room temperature with vegetarian food.

Serves 6.

KHEERA KA KACHORI
Cucumber-stuffed Semolina Pancakes

This remarkably inventive recipe is from the state of Murshidabad, where the Marwari community created this preparation for stuffed pancakes. The Maharajah of Murshidabad was the Muslim ruler married to a Jewish woman of the Calcutta community during my tenure of residence in Calcutta. The Marwaris are devout Hindus. This is a labor-intensive dish, typical of Marwari cooking.

THE CUCUMBER
> 2 *pounds Kirby cucumbers, peeled*

THE DOUGH
> 3 *cups semolina* (soojee)
> *1 cup white flour*
> *1/2 cup whole wheat flour*
> *5 tablespoons* ghee *(clarified butter) or butter, melted*
> *1/2 teaspoon salt*
> *1 cup reserved cucumber liquid*

THE YOGHURT
> 2 *1/2 cups yoghurt*

THE PANCAKES
> *1 teaspoon hot red chili powder*
> *2 teaspoons ground cumin, lightly toasted*
> *1 tablespoon ground cinnamon*
> *1/2 teaspoon salt*
> *Oil for deep-frying*

1. Prepare the cucumbers: Grate the cucumbers on a coarse grater. Put them in a cloth kitchen towel and squeeze as much liquid as possible out into a bowl. Reserve 1 cup liquid. There will be about 3 cups cucumber pulp.
2. Prepare the dough: Mix all the ingredients together to form a

firm dough. Knead the dough for a few minutes, cover it with a damp cloth, and let rest for 1 hour.

3. Prepare the yoghurt: Put the yoghurt in a cloth bag, tie it over the sink, and let drain for several hours. You can also put many layers of kitchen towels in a bowl, pour in the yoghurt, and let stand for 1 hour. The towels will absorb the liquid, leaving about 2 cups thick yoghurt. Set aside.

4. Prepare the pancakes: Mix the cucumber pulp with the chili powder, cumin, and cinnamon. (The salt must be added at the moment of stuffing.)

5. Take 1 heaping tablespoon of the dough and roll it out into a thin pancake 5 inches in diameter. Roll out another pancake.

6. Put 2 heaping tablespoons of the cucumber mixture in the center of one pancake and sprinkle with salt. Moisten the edge of the pancake all around with water. Cover with a second pancake and press the edges firmly to seal. Pinch the edge and fold it over, then continue to pinch and fold all the way around. Prick the top 3 or 4 times with the tines of a fork so that moisture can escape. Roll out, stuff, seal, and prick pancakes with the remaining dough and stuffing in the same way.

7. Heat the oil in a wok or large skillet and deep-fry the stuffed pancakes, a few at a time, over low heat until brown, about 3 minutes. Drain briefly on paper towels. Serve warm or at room temperature as a snack or as part of a meal.

Makes 30 stuffed pancakes.

BHINDI KA BAJA
Simply Fried Okra

> Okra takes only a few minutes to cook. That way it retains its shape and does not disintegrate. This is a very popular method of preparation for a very popular vegetable.

1/2 pound fresh okra
2 tablespoons peanut oil
1/4 teaspoon cuminseed
1/8 teaspoon hing (asafoetida; see Glossary)
1/4 teaspoon turmeric
1/2 teaspoon salt

1. Trim both ends of the okra and cut into 1/4-inch pieces.
2. Prepare the *baghar:* Heat the oil in a wok or skillet. Add the cuminseed and *hing* and stir-fry over low heat for 5 seconds. Add the okra and stir-fry for 1/2 minute. Add the turmeric and salt and stir-fry rapidly for 1 minute. Then fry the okra for 3 or 4 minutes to lightly brown. Serve warm.

Serves 6, with other dishes.

VARIATION
BHINDI KA DUBDABA
Sour and Hot Okra

1 recipe Bhindi Ka Baja (above) fried until light brown
2 teaspoons tamarind paste dissolved in 2 tablespoons water and strained
2 teaspoons ground coriander
1/4 teaspoon hot red chili powder

After the okra has turned light brown, add the tamarind liquid, coriander, and chili powder. Stir-fry 2 minutes until the liquid has evaporated. Serve warm.

Serves 6.

BHINDI KA
BHARAWN
Tamarind-stuffed Okra

> *Bhindi* are okra, also called lady's fingers and sometimes in Calcutta, *bamia*. They are seasonal and extremely popular considering, after all, that they are a member of the cotton family. The acid flavor of tamarind is an attractive foil to the characteristic taste of okra.

1/2 pound fresh okra
  1 tablespoon tamarind paste dissolved in 3 tablespoons water and strained
  1 tablespoon ground coriander
  1 teaspoon hot red chili powder
1/2 teaspoon salt
1/4 teaspoon turmeric
  2 tablespoons peanut oil
1/2 teaspoon cuminseed
1/8 teaspoon hing (asafoetida; see Glossary)
1/4 cup water

1. Trim both ends of the okra. Cut a 2-inch slit from top to bottom on each so that you can stuff the center.
2. Mix together the tamarind liquid, coriander, chili powder, salt, and turmeric. Stuff each okra with about 1/2 teaspoon of this paste.
3. Heat the oil in a skillet to prepare the *baghar*. Add the cuminseed and *hing* and sizzle the mixture over low heat for 5 seconds. Add the stuffed okra, one by one, in layers and dribble the water into the skillet. Cover and fry over low heat for 15 minutes, enough time to tenderize the okra and evaporate nearly all the liquid. Serve warm.

Serves 6 with other dishes.

ALOO DUM
Whole Potatoes and Spice

There are two methods of preparing the *aloo dum*, one is with sauce and the other is a dry fry. I had both styles during my residence in Calcutta, but somehow I lean toward the dry as the potatoes can be picked up with your fingers and eaten as an appetizer with drinks. I've provided directions for both styles below.

     2   *pounds small potatoes, 2 inches in length*
     3   *tablespoons peanut oil*
   1/2   *teaspoon cuminseed*
   1/8   *teaspoon* hing *(asafoetida; see Glossary)*
     2   *bay leaves*
     1   *whole hot red dried chili*
   1/2   *teaspoon turmeric*
   1/2   *teaspoon salt*
     2   *tablespoons ground coriander*
     1   *cup water*
1/2–1   *teaspoon hot red chili powder*
     1   *tablespoon chopped fresh coriander (Chinese parsley)*

1. Boil the potatoes in their skins until soft but with some firmness. Cool and peel. Set aside.
2. Prepare the *baghar:* Heat the oil in a pan, add the cuminseed, *hing*, bay leaves, and whole chili. Fry over low heat for 5 seconds as the spices sizzle.
3. Add the potatoes and stir-fry for 10 minutes. Then add the turmeric, salt, ground coriander, and 2 tablespoons of the water to moisten the mixture. Stir everything to combine for 1 minute.
4. Add the chili powder and the remaining water. Bring to a boil, cook for 5 minutes, uncovered, and remove the pan from the heat. Sprinkle with the coriander.

     Should you prefer a dry fry, then continue to simmer the potatoes until nearly all the liquid has evaporated. Serve warm.

Serves 6–8.

MOOLEE KA SAAG
Spinach and Spice

This is one of the most popular vegetarian stir-fry dishes in Calcutta, where a continuous supply of green leaf vegetables is available, especially during the monsoon season. Tamarind, cumin, coriander, and hot chili glorify this tasty preparation.

  1 *tablespoon peanut oil*
1/4 *teaspoon cuminseed*
  1 *small fresh or dried hot, whole red chili*
1/2 *pound finely chopped spinach or Swiss chard*
1/4 *teaspoon turmeric*
1/4 *teaspoon salt*
  2 *teaspoons tamarind paste dissolved in 3 tablespoons water and strained*
  2 *teaspoons ground coriander*
1/4 *teaspoon hot red chili powder*

1. Prepare the *baghar:* Heat the oil in a wok or skillet, add the cuminseed and whole chili, and stir-fry for 10 seconds. Add the spinach, turmeric, and salt and continue to stir-fry for 2 minutes.
2. Add the strained tamarind liquid, coriander, and chili powder and stir-fry over moderate heat for about 3 minutes to evaporate the liquid. Serve warm or at room temperature.

Serves 4–6.

VARIATION
LAL SAAG
Red Spinach and Spice

Use 1/2 pound red Asian spinach, found in Asian markets, instead of the green variety. In this case, do not add the tamarind juice, coriander, or chili powder.

DAHI BURA
Long Beans in Yoghurt Sauce

Chinese long beans, also known in Asia as *loobia*, are frequently found in New York City's Chinatown and in Asian groceries as well. They are twelve to fourteen inches in length, come in different shades of green, and grow on low bushes or as climbing plants. I have seen them in Indonesia and Burma as well as in India.

1/2 pound Chinese long beans
1 tablespoon peanut oil
1/4 teaspoon cuminseed
1/8 teaspoon hing *(asafoetida; see Glossary)*
1/4 teaspoon turmeric
1/2 teaspoon salt
1 cup yoghurt whipped together with 1/4 teaspoon chick-pea flour
1/4 cup water
1/4 teaspoon hot red chili powder
1/2 teaspoon ground cumin
1/4 teaspoon ground cinnamon

1. Trim the ends of the beans and cut them into 1/4-inch pieces.
2. Prepare the *baghar:* Heat the oil in a pan, add the cuminseed and *hing*, and stir-fry over moderate heat for 10 seconds. Add the beans, turmeric, and salt and stir-fry for 3 minutes.
3. Add the yoghurt mixture and continue to stir for 5 minutes. Add the water, chili powder, cumin, and cinnamon and simmer another minute. Test the beans for tenderness and remove the pan from the heat. Serve warm or at room temperature.

Serves 6.

KIDGEREE
Rice, Spices, and Water Chestnuts

This extraordinary combination of rice, spices, water chestnuts, saffron, and almonds is an example of the many convolutions of the Marwari cooks of Murshidabad, a city about 150 miles north of Calcutta. Nuances and dimensions are important for this preparation, which depends upon the sensitive hand of the vegetarian cook.

When I lived in Calcutta, the *pani phal wallah* (water chestnut sellers) were parked around the entrance to the sprawling New Market, selling the horned seeds with their thick green skin that is peeled away to reveal the white, sweet, crunchy nut inside. These are not the Chinese water chestnuts, a different botanical group, but Chinese water chestnuts can be used as a substitute. The *pani phal* are attractive aquatic plants that produce the water chestnut (*Trapa natans*), which is taken from the ponds during the monsoon season when there is plenty of water everywhere.

4 tablespoons ghee *(clarified butter) or butter, melted*
1 recipe *Mardiea* baghar *(pages 49-50)*
3 cups *water chestnuts* (pani phal; see Glossary), *cut into 1/2-inch pieces*
1 teaspoon salt
1/4 teaspoon turmeric
1 teaspoon cuminseed
10 whole almonds
3 inches cinnamon stick, broken up
4 cardamom pods
4 whole cloves, broken up
1 1/2 cups yoghurt
3 threads saffron
1 teaspoon garam masala *(see Glossary)*
2 cups cooked rice

THE SECOND BAGHAR
2 tablespoons ghee *or butter, melted*
3 cardamom pods
3 whole cloves

1/8 teaspoon hing *(asafoetida; see Glossary)*
1/2 teaspoon cuminseed
1/2 teaspoon hot red chili powder

1. Heat the *ghee* or melted butter in a pan over low heat and add the Mardiea *baghar.* Stir-fry a few seconds until brown. Add the water chestnuts and stir well. Add the salt and turmeric, cover the pan, and cook for 5 minutes, stirring occasionally.
2. Prepare a ground paste with the cuminseeds, almonds, cinnamon stick, cardamom pods, and cloves. Grind until smooth, adding a tablespoon or two of water to moisten the mixture.
3. Mix the paste with the yoghurt. Add the saffron and *garam masala* and stir well. Add to the cooked rice in a pan and mix again. Place over low heat to keep warm.
4. Prepare the second *baghar:* Heat the *ghee* or melted butter in a small pan or skillet and add the cardamom pods, cloves, *hing,* cuminseed, and chili powder and sizzle for about 10 seconds.
5. Pour the mixture over the rice and cover the pan immediately so that the aroma does not escape. When ready to serve, stir briefly. Serve warm with papadum and Mardiea (page 49).

Serves 6 or more.

DAHI BARA
Lentil Balls with Yoghurt Sauce

Many Marwari dishes can be served as snacks or as one of several dishes for lunch, dinner, or at celebrations. *Dahi bara* is one of them.

THE LENTILS

1 cup moong dal
1 cup urad dal *(black lentils)*
1/2 teaspoon coriander seed
1 teaspoon hot red chili powder
2 cups ghee *(clarified butter) or butter, melted*
A large pan of 8 cups cold water mixed with 1 tablespoon salt
2 cups yoghurt

TOPPING SPICE

1 tablespoon cuminseed
1/2 teaspoon hot red chili powder
1/2 teaspoon salt
1/4 teaspoon ground ginger

1. Prepare the lentils: Soak the *moong* and *urad dal* together in water for 6–8 hours. Drain.
2. Process the lentils to a smooth paste, transfer to a bowl, and with a wooden spoon stir rapidly in one direction only for 5 minutes. Add the coriander seed and chili powder and mix.
3. Heat the *ghee* or butter in a wok or skillet. Take about 1 heaping tablespoon of the lentil mix and drop it in. Brown over moderate heat for 2–3 minutes. Scoop out and put in the pan of salted cold water. (The balls will sink to the bottom.) Prepare all the lentil mixture this way.
4. Drain off the water, gently squeeze out the liquid in each ball, and arrange on a serving plate.
5. Make the topping spice: Toast the cuminseed in a dry skillet

until light brown. Grind to a powder. Combine with all the remaining spices.

6. Pour the yoghurt over the lentil balls and sprinkle with the topping spice. Serve at room temperature.

Serves 6.

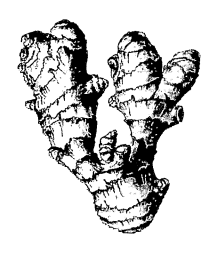

L Ɐ P P S I
Cracked Wheat Sweet

This popular sweet porridge is served during the Jain Marwari auspicious occasions, such as Holi and Diwali, at weddings, or special religious observances, or for the arrival of a new male baby in the house. When the baby is one month old, *lappsi* is prepared. When the boy is one year old, he is given his first haircut (which is to say until he is completely bald) in the Hindu temple and *lappsi* is served for this happy occasion, too.

During the Durga Puja, the festival to the god Durga, the Marwari offer this sweet to Durga.

It is interesting to note that the Marwari, who originally came from Rajasthan, a wheat-producing region, are wheat-eaters, although they now live in Bengal, a region of rice-eaters. This aromatic, delicious, and rich sweet is prepared with bulghur, cracked wheat.

1 1/4 cups ghee *(clarified butter) or butter, melted*
  1 cup coarse bulgur
  3 cups water
  1 cup sugar
  6 almonds
  6 cardamom pods, husks removed

1. Heat the *ghee* in a pan and add the bulgur. Stir continuously over low heat for 5 minutes. (The bulghur will turn a reddish brown color.)
2. Add the water, cover the pan, and cook for 15 minutes. Add the sugar, stir well, and continue to cook over low heat for 1/2 hour, stirring frequently.
3. Very coarsely grind together the almonds and cardamom pods and sprinkle them over the mixture. Serve warm or at room temperature.

Serves 6.

ĀTĀ KĀ HĀLWĀ
Whole Wheat Sweet

Halwa is usually served as a breakfast food. It could also be enjoyed at tea or coffee hour. It is a thick concoction with a sweet nut-like flavor. The Marwaris like *ghee*, perhaps to excess according to our calculations. I suggest that in the event you have qualms about so much butterfat, then reduce the amount by half. The recipe will still work well.

1 *cup whole wheat flour*
1 *cup* ghee *(clarified butter) or butter, melted*
1/2 *cup sugar*
2 *cups water*
2 *tablespoons sliced blanched almonds and 1/4 teaspoon rosewater for garnish .*

1. Mix the flour and *ghee* together in a pan or skillet. Stir-fry the mixture over low heat until the color changes to a rich brown, about 5 minutes.
2. Add the sugar, stir a minute, and add the water. Stir well and simmer for about 10 minutes, stirring continuously. Turn out into a serving dish and garnish with the almonds and rose-water. Serve warm.

Serves 4.

VARIATIONS
SOOJEE KĀ HĀLWĀ
Semolina Sweet

1 *cup semolina* (soojee)
1/2 *cup* ghee *(clarified butter) or butter, melted*
1/2 *cup sugar*
1 *cup water*
1 *tablespoon raisins*
2 *teaspoons sliced blanched almonds for garnish*

1. Mix the semolina and *ghee* together in a pan. Stir-fry over low heat until the color changes to a rich brown, about 4 minutes.
2. Add the sugar and water, mix well, add the raisins and cook for 10 minutes. Turn out into a serving dish and garnish with the almonds. Serve warm or at room temperature.

Serves 4.

VARIATIONS
BADAM KA HALWA
Almond Sweet

1 cup blanched almonds
1 tablespoon water
1/4 cup ghee *(clarified butter) or butter, melted*
1/2 cup sugar

1. Grind the almonds very fine in a processor, adding the water to moisten. You should have an almond paste.
2. Heat the *ghee* in a wok or skillet, add the almond paste, and stir-fry over low heat until the color turns beige. Do not overcook. Add the sugar and continue to stir-fry until well blended and the sugar has dissolved, about 5 minutes. Turn out into a serving dish. Serve at room temperature with tea or coffee.

Serves 4.

POUA PATTI CHAI
(ALSO CHAI MASALA)
Spiced Tea

There are several varieties of spiced tea served around Calcutta. This *chai masala* was served to me for the first time and innumerable times afterward once I had become accustomed to its unaccustomed and exotic flavor. Well spiced with the emphasis on cardamom and ginger, laced with sugar to taste, and generally on the sweet side, the tea is sipped rather than drunk. Sometimes a bay leaf is thrown into the brew, but this is an optional choice as it is not to everyone's taste and not to mine. The Marwaris will also add several saffron threads, which adds a note of luxury and a pleasant aroma.

Mural. Hindu Temple, Puri, India

       2 cups milk
     1–2 tablespoons sugar, to taste
       5 cardamom pods, cracked with a mallet
       1 small bay leaf (optional)
          1/2-inch piece fresh ginger, smashed
       2 tablespoons Darjeeling, Assam, or other tea leaves

Put the milk, sugar, cardamom, bay leaf if used, and ginger into a pan and bring to a boil over moderate heat. Add the tea leaves and bring to a boil again, removing the pan from the heat and swirling it back and forth as the milk foams, mixing the brew. Do this 3 times. Serve the tea in demitasse cups.

Serves 6.

NOTE: One time I saw this procedure done in a tiny public tea shop. The cook, sitting cross-legged under a banyan tree, lifted and swirled the tea pan, with its foaming hot milk and tea mixture, like a circus performer.

⁘ 3 ⁘

THE JEWISH WAY WITH
PICKLES AND CHUTNEYS

DURING THE eighteenth and nineteenth centuries a trickle of Jewish traders filtered into India from the ancient city of Baghdad, Iraq, where Jews had lived for several thousand years. They settled in Bombay and Calcutta, where they established communities with schools, synagogues, a rabbi—a Judaic way of life that was identifiable as being Jewish.

Around them were the native Hindus, living out their own lives, who considered these outsiders just another caste that was separated from them by their cultural idiosyncrasies.

I am principally concerned with the Baghdadi Jews of Calcutta, where I lived and have visited for many years. My acquaintance with the Baghdadis has had a profound effect on my diet for one thing and on my life: I have an enormous interest in this talented community.

Calcutta, the city itself, was established by Job Charnock for the British East India Company on August 24, 1690. Rudyard Kipling in a few imperishable stanzas wrote:

> *Where the cholera, the cyclone, and the Crow*
> *Come and go;*
> *Stands a City—Charnock chose it—packed away*
> *Near a Bay—*
> *By the sewage rendered fetid, by the sewer*
> *Made impure,*

Not much has changed since those lines were penned in the middle of the nineteenth century, except that the city is now swamped by a horrendous increase in population. Yet the Jews prospered.

The New Market Clock Tower, Calcutta

The celebrated patisserie and bakery of the Nahoum family is one of the adornments of the equally famous New Market in the center of Calcutta. Since its establishment in 1874 the New Market has been the most renowned of Calcutta's shopping markets. Here one can buy anything from jewelry to meat, fish, saris and other fabrics, to fruits and vegetables, and one hundred other items for daily use.

Nahoum's is still going strong after almost a century, with its famous fruitcake, which is exported to old India hands whose nostalgia for the New Market, "warts and all," is assuaged after the first bite.

There is a plaque outside the New Market office that states: This market building is an extension of the one on the west which was built in 1874 by the justices of peace. Sir Stuart Hogg, being chairman of the justices, the market was named after him." In December 1985, a serious fire destroyed about one third of the market. A report in one of the Calcutta English language newspapers stated that one of the shopkeepers in the market believed that Halley's Comet passing near the earth at that time was responsible for the conflagration. But Nahoum's was not damaged.

Helen Nahoum presides over the kosher kitchen in her home a few hundred yards from the New Market. She and her brother Norman are the guardians of their family's century-old recipes of chutneys and pickles. To my knowledge, they had not ever been recorded and when the invitation came to record them before

Helen and Norman Nahoum at the New Market, Calcutta

they disappeared into the twentieth century, they were honored to accept.

The chutneys and pickles are homemade in small quantities, then matured and bottled. There is no industrial complex here, only authentic Jewish preserves, prepared in modest quantities, with the freshest ingredients and spices. It is this control that has produced the marvelous assortment of table condiments sold in the Nahoum bakery. The public benefits, and there is the continuity of an old culinary process kept active by an ancient family and community.

RULES OF THE GAME

There is a special ambiance in Calcutta when preparing chutneys and pickles. The climate there, which is hot and humid most of the year, is not conducive to the easy preparation of this type of method of preserving fruits and vegetables. Not all items are seasonal; mangoes, for instance are, and preserving them in chutney is a way of enjoying them at another time. However, there is a snake in paradise, and much care must be taken in India (less in temperate climates) so that the preserves do not deteriorate. Here is a list of the points most important to me:

1. Everything included in the preserves must be seasonally fresh, without blemish, and the spices, especially, should be freshly ground and toasted when required.
2. There are fresh pickles that do not require lengthy maturing before they can be consumed. One or two days are all that may be required. A preserve cooked with mustard or peanut oil may include sufficient oil so that the pickle is covered when bottled. About 1/4 inch of oil on the top preserves the pickle from contamination. Without this protective cover, the pickle could decay in the bone-melting heat of Calcutta.

   Vinegar is crucial to the good taste of a preserve. Cider vinegar found in all supermarkets is quite adequate, and I have indicated this in the recipes that follow. White vinegar, which is sometimes used for rinsing produce, is secondary in importance. Vinegar is also a preservative.
4. I was cautioned to use a wooden spoon in all of the cooking processes. Wood is neutral and preferred by Calcutta cooks.

Tasting a batch of chutney off the mixing spoon, then returning the spoon to the pot is courting disaster (according to my
teacher) as it may contaminate the entire batch.

5. The preparation of mango preserves is truly surprising. Sliced
   Sweet Mango Chutney (page 83) and, in fact, all the others
   use hard, green, sour mangoes, whereas one might be led to
   believe that sweet mango chutney is made with sweet ripe
   mangoes. Not at all!

6. Hot red chili powder is sometimes used in generous quantities
   in the making of pickles. I suggest that a judicious amount be
   added instead, according to your personal preference.

7. Chutney and pickles should be bottled in glass jars that contain about 1 pound of the preserve and 1 3/4 to 2 cups contents. (This will vary with the bulk.) As long as the contents
   are covered with 1/4 inch of oil, then they may be considered
   to be preserved. I always refrigerate the jars after opening. Although I do not state it on the recipes that follow, the jars and
   lids have been sterilized according to modern techniques.

LIME CHUTNEY WITH PLUMS AND DATES

Indian limes (*nimbu*) are not available in the United States. They are the same or similar to the Key lime of Florida or the small round yellow lemons found in Guatemala and Mexico. For this chutney substitute the small Key limes of Florida.

12 *whole green limes*
2 *tablespoons salt*
1/2 *pound fresh ginger, peeled and sliced*
1/2 *pound garlic, peeled and sliced*
1 *pound pitted dates*
1 *pound firm red sour plums, quartered and pits discarded*
4 *cups sugar*
1 *cup cider vinegar*
1 *tablespoon red chili powder*

1. Toss together the limes and salt. Store the salted limes in a glass or stone jar in the sun for 12 days, shaking the jar now and then during this time. Quarter the limes and remove the pits. Reserve the salted liquid.
2. In a food processor grind together the ginger and garlic with 1/2 cup of the vinegar.
3. Put the salted limes, dates, plums, sugar, remaining vinegar, and chili powder in the processor and grind them together coarsely. Add the reserved salted liquid to moisten the mixture.
4. Put the chopped mixture in a pan, add the ginger-garlic paste, and cook over low heat, stirring frequently, for about 1/2 hour, until very thick.

    Transfer the chutney to a glass or stone jar, cover, and let mature for 1 week when it will be ready to taste. Bottle it in 5 jars.

Makes about 1 quart.

MANGO CHUTNEY
WITH RAISINS

5 *pounds hard, green mangoes, peeled, seeds discarded, and the pulp sliced*
1 *quart cider vinegar*
6 *ounces fresh ginger, peeled and sliced*
6 *ounces garlic, peeled and sliced*
1/2 *pound golden raisins*
1/4 *pound yellow mustard seeds, ground fine*
1/4 *pound tamarind paste, soaked in 1/4 cup vinegar for 1/2 hour and*
   strained
1 1/4 *pounds sugar*
1 *teaspoon salt*

1. In a food processor process all the ingredients to a smooth paste.
2. Put the paste in a large pan and cook it over moderate heat, stirring constantly, for 10 minutes to prevent it from scorching. (This chutney has a paste consistency and is not watery.) Cool completely.

   Store in 5 bottles. Allow 2 days to mature before tasting.

Makes 1 1/2 quarts.

MANGO KASUNDI CHUTNEY

This is not a cooked chutney, but one in which all the ingredients are raw, so that the longer the storage before tasting the more intense the flavor.

3 pounds hard, green mangoes (about 3 large)
2 tablespoons white vinegar
2 tablespoons red chili powder
2 tablespoons thinly sliced peeled fresh ginger
2 tablespoons thinly sliced garlic
2 tablespoons yellow mustard seeds, coarsely crushed
1 cup salt
2 cups cider vinegar

1. Peel the mangoes and slice the pulp into thin long pieces. Discard the seeds. Rinse the pulp in the white vinegar.
2. Mix the mango pieces with the remaining ingredients.
   Store in 4 or 5 bottles and leave them in the sun or in a warm place in the kitchen for 4 days or 1 week if it is overcast.

Makes about 1 1/2 quarts.

NOTE In several of the chutney and pickle recipes in the Nahoum collection, one of the instructions is to rinse the fruit or pulp in white vinegar. Originally, I was told that the rinse was done in a "cheap" vinegar, a white one, not the more flavorful cider vinegar. However, if desired, one can use cider vinegar for rinsing as well.

MANGO SAUCE

3 pounds mango pulp from 4 pounds hard, green, sour mangoes
2 pounds tamarind paste
1/2 cup water
1 pound garlic, peeled
1 pound fresh ginger, peeled and chopped coarse
1 pound golden raisins
1/2 cup salt
1/2 cup red chili powder, or less to taste
1 cup cider vinegar

1. Peel the mangoes, slice off the pulp, and discard the seeds. Weigh the pulp. (I suggest 4 pounds whole mangoes to produce the 3 pounds of pulp needed.) Grind the pulp in a food processor to a smooth paste.
2. Soak the tamarind paste in the water for 1/2 hour, loosening the pulp with your fingers. Press the tamarind through a metal strainer and reserve the thick paste. Discard the seeds and fibres.
3. Grind the garlic, ginger, raisins, mango paste, tamarind paste, salt, chili powder, and vinegar in the processor. Pour the mixture into a glass jar and let stand for 1 week at room temperature.
4. Strain the mixture through cheesecloth into a pan, pressing out the liquid firmly. Discard the pulp.
5. Bring the liquid to a boil and simmer over low heat for 5–10 minutes. (The sauce should have the consistency of tomato ketchup.) Cool completely.

   Store in 4 or 5 jars. The sauce may be used immediately with curries, rice, or with any kind of traditional Jewish cooking of Calcutta.

Makes about 1 quart.

SLICED SWEET
MANGO CHUTNEY

Here is perhaps the most popular of all Indian chutneys and pickles.

  5 *large green, sour mangoes, peeled (5 pounds)*
  4 *pounds sugar*
1 1/2 *cups cider vinegar*
  3/4 *cup salt*
  4 *ounces garlic, peeled and sliced thin*
  4 *ounces fresh ginger, peeled and cut into round slices*
4 or 5 *whole dried hot red chilis*

Cut the pulp from the mangoes into slices about 3 inches long and 1 inch wide. Combine the mangoes and all the remaining ingredients in a large pan, stir well, and cook over moderate/low heat until the mixture thickens, about 1/2 hour. Stir constantly to avoid scorching. The chutney will have a jamlike consistency. Taste for salt and sugar and adjust accordingly. Always use a clean dry wooden or plastic spoon to avoid contaminating the whole batch. Cool well.

Store the chutney in several glass jars with tight covers for 2 days before tasting.

Makes about 1 quart.

TOMATO CHUTNEY

6 pounds firm but ripe fresh tomatoes (about 12 medium)
1/4 cup white vinegar
1/4 pound fresh ginger, peeled and sliced
1/4 pound garlic, peeled and sliced
 1 cup cider vinegar
 1 cup peanut oil
 1 tablespoon red chili powder
 1 tablespoon salt
 2 cups sugar
 2 teaspoons turmeric

1. Rinse the tomatoes in the white vinegar, then quarter them.
2. In a food processor, process the ginger and garlic in the cider vinegar to a relatively smooth paste.
3. Warm the oil in a pan and add the ginger-garlic paste, chili powder, salt, sugar, and turmeric and simmer over low heat for 1 minute, stirring with a wooden spoon.
4. Add the tomatoes and cook until the mixture becomes thick, about 1/2 hour, to the consistency of thick jam. (Tomatoes are full of water and it must evaporate.) Cool, transfer to a glass or stone jar, and cover. Let mature 2 days before bottling.
    Divide among 6 bottles.

NOTE: Each bottle holds about 3/4 pound chutney and contains roughly 1 3/4–2 cups.

TOMATO KASUNDI

4 pounds firm, not-too-ripe fresh red tomatoes
1 cup cider vinegar
1 pound dark brown sugar
3 tablespoons raisins
1/2 cup peanut oil
1 inch fresh ginger, peeled and ground to a paste
4 cloves garlic, peeled and ground to a paste
3/4 teaspoon turmeric
1 teaspoon mustard seed, lightly toasted and coarsely ground
1 teaspoon red chili powder
1 teaspoon cuminseed, lightly toasted and ground
1 tablespoon salt

1. Blanch the tomatoes briefly in boiling water, cool, and remove the skins. Cut in half.
2. Mix the vinegar, brown sugar, and raisins together in a pan. Bring to a boil, remove from the heat, and cool.
3. Heat the oil in a wok or pan, add the ginger and garlic pastes, turmeric, mustard seeds, chili powder, cuminseed, and salt. Stir-fry over low heat for 2 minutes. Add the vinegar mixture and tomatoes and cook over moderate heat for about 20 minutes, or until the mixture reduces to a not-too-thick jam.

   Cool completely and store in 5 or 6 bottles. Let stand 2 days before tasting.

Makes 1 quart.

BAMBOO PICKLE

During the monsoon season in Calcutta, fresh bamboo shoots are harvested. As they are a rarity in the United States, canned bamboo shoots,
which are readily available, have been called for in this recipe.

2 *pounds canned bamboo shoots*
1/2 *teaspoon turmeric*
2 *tablespoons peeled fresh ginger, ground to a paste*
2 *tablespoons garlic, ground to a paste with 2 tablespoons cider vinegar*
1/4 *teaspoon ground cumin*
1 *pound sugar*
1 *teaspoon salt*
1/2 *teaspoon ground mustard seed*
1/2 *teaspoon red chili powder*
1 1/2 *cups peanut oil*

1. Rinse the bamboo shoots very well in cold water. Drain and
   cut into julienne slices. In a pan cover them with water, add the
   turmeric, and bring to a boil. Drain immediately and cool. Put
   the shoots in a kitchen towel and gently squeeze out the liquid. Do not press the bamboo shoots too firmly or twist the
   towel as the shoots will break. Spread out on a tray to dry for
   1 day.

2. Put all the remaining ingredients, except the bamboo shoots,
   in a pan and simmer slowly over low heat for 15 minutes as the
   mixture comes to a boil. Add the bamboo shoots and continue
   to simmer for 10 minutes. Cool completely.

   Bottle the pickle. Make certain that at least 1/4 inch oil covers the pickle at all times. Put the pickle in the sun for 1 week.
   The pickle is now ready to eat.

NOTES: Do not press the bamboo shoots too firmly as it will break them
up.
   An enamel pan is an ideal implement to use when preparing this
pickle.

FRESH CABBAGE
PICKLE

1 1/2 *pounds shredded fresh cabbage*
  2 *tablespoons plus 1/2 teaspoon salt*
  1 *inch fresh ginger, peeled and chopped fine*
  6 *cloves garlic, peeled and chopped fine*
  2 *sprigs flat-leaf parsley, chopped fine*
  1 *teaspoon peanut oil*
4–6 *small hot green chilis, to taste, sliced very thin*
  1 *cup cider vinegar*
  1 *tablespoon sugar*

1. Toss the cabbage with the 2 tablespoons salt and set aside for 20 minutes. Put the cabbage in a cloth kitchen towel and very firmly squeeze out the liquid. Rinse the cabbage with cold water and again firmly squeeze out the liquid.
2. In a bowl mix together the cabbage, ginger, garlic, parsley, and oil and add the chilis.
3. Combine the vinegar, sugar, remaining 1/2 teaspoon salt, and cabbage mixture in a wok or large pan and quickly bring to a boil, stirring constantly. Remove the pan from the heat immediately. Cool. Store the pickle in a glass jar with a tight cover for 1 day before tasting. Refrigerate after tasting. The pickle can be refrigerated for up to 1 week.

Makes 1 quart.

CAULIFLOWER PICKLE

    3 large heads cauliflower (about 6 pounds), well rinsed and cut into
       1-inch florets
   10 small whole hot green chilis with a 1-inch slit in the side of each
    2 tablespoons salt
 1 1/2 cups peanut oil
  1/4 pound fresh ginger, peeled and sliced
  1/4 pound garlic, peeled and sliced
    2 cups cider vinegar
    2 teaspoons ground fenugreek
    1 tablespoon yellow mustard seed, ground
 3 or 4 tablespoons hot red chili powder, to taste
    1 tablespoon ground cumin
    1 teaspoon turmeric
  1/2 cup sugar

1. Toss the cauliflower and chilis with the salt, arrange on a tray,
   and dry for 1 day at room temperature.
2. The next day, bring the oil in a wok or pan to a boil over low
   heat. Cool for 15 minutes.
3. In a food processor, chop the ginger and garlic with 1/2 cup of
   the vinegar to a relatively smooth paste.
4. Add the paste to the oil with the fenugreek, mustard powder,
   chili powder, cumin, turmeric, and sugar and simmer for 3 minutes, stirring continuously.
5. Add the remaining vinegar and bring the mixture to a boil.
   Add the cauliflower and chilis, mix well, and cook for 5 minutes. The florets should remain crunchy.
      Put the pickle in a glass or stone jar, making sure that oil
   covers the cauliflower. Let the pickle mature for 1 week before
   bottling in 8 jars. Cover the jars with both plastic wrap and a
   tight cover.

Makes about 2 quarts.

FRESH CUCUMBER PICKLE

6 firm, plump Kirby cucumbers (1 1/2 pounds), sliced thin
2 tablespoons plus 1/2 teaspoon salt
1 1/2 inches fresh ginger, peeled and chopped fine
8 cloves garlic, peeled and chopped fine
2 sprigs fresh mint or flat-leaf parsley, chopped fine
4–6 small hot green chilis, to taste, sliced very thin
1 cup cider vinegar
1 tablespoon sugar

1. Toss the cucumber slices with the 2 tablespoons salt and set aside for 20 minutes. Put the cucumbers in a cloth kitchen towel and very firmly squeeze out the liquid. Rinse the slices in cold water and again firmly squeeze out the liquid.
2. In a bowl mix together the cucumbers, ginger, garlic, and mint or parsley and add the chili peppers.
3. In a pan bring the vinegar, sugar, and the remaining 1/2 teaspoon salt to a boil. Cool and pour over the cucumber mixture. Store the pickle in a glass jar with a tight cover for 1 day before tasting. Refrigerate after tasting. The pickle can be refrigerated for about 1 week.

Makes about 1 quart.

FRESH ASSORTED
VEGETABLE PICKLE

This is a fresh garden pickle that does not require long maturing before tasting.

1 tablespoon peanut oil
1 cup cider vinegar
1 teaspoon salt
1 tablespoon sugar
1 inch fresh ginger, peeled and sliced
8 whole cloves garlic, peeled
6 small whole green chilis
1 teaspoon hot mustard seed, coarsely ground
3 pounds assorted firm vegetables (see Note)

Put the oil in a pan, add the vinegar, salt, sugar, ginger, garlic, chili, mustard seed, and pearl onions if used. Simmer over moderate heat for 2 minutes; add all the vegetables. Bring the mixture to a boil, stirring constantly, and remove from the heat immediately. Cool. Store the pickle, covered, in a glass or stone jar. Set aside 1 day before tasting. Refrigerate after tasting. The pickle can be refrigerated for 1 week or more.

Makes about 2 quarts.

Note Use 5 or 6 of the following vegetables for a total of 3 pounds.

Pearl onions (not more than 1/2 inch in diameter each)
Cauliflower (cut into 1-inch florets)
Carrots (cut into 1/4-inch-thick diagonal slices)
String beans (cut into 1-inch lengths)
White turnips (cut into thin 1-inch pieces)
Chayote (peeled and cut into 1-inch pieces, 1/4 inch thick)
Green (hard) **papaya** (peeled and cut into small pieces, 1/4 inch thick)

PICKLED LADY'S FINGERS

In Calcutta the British called okra, "lady's fingers" as the shape of the vegetable pod reminded them of that. The Baghdadi Jews called okra *bamiya*, which is Arabic. Okra is the botanical name and it shall be called that here.

1 pound plump okra, each 3 inches long
2 teaspoons salt
2 tablespoons chopped garlic
2 tablespoons chopped fresh ginger
6 sprigs finely chopped mint, fresh coriander (Chinese parsley), or flat-leaf parsley leaves
2 tablespoons finely chopped small hot green chili
1 1/2 cups cider vinegar
1 tablespoon sugar

1. Trim off the top of each okra. Cut each okra open almost its entire length but do not split it open entirely. Take a good pinch of salt and rub it into the interior of each okra. Set aside for 20 minutes. The okra will soften and become easier to fill.
2. Mix together the garlic, ginger, mint or other herb, and chili. Carefully fill each okra with 1/2 teaspoon of the mixture and close it. Arrange the okra in a flat layer in a jar large enough to hold all of them. Any leftover spice mixture can be put into the jar as well.
3. In a pan bring the vinegar and sugar to a rapid boil. Cool and pour into the jar. The vinegar mixture must cover the okra to preserve it. If there isn't enough, bring a few tablespoons additional vinegar to a boil with some sugar, let cool, and pour it over the pickle.

   Let the pickle mature, covered, 5 days before tasting and bottling. Refrigerate after tasting.

Makes about 1 1/2 quarts.

PRESERVED LEMONS

Indian lemons are green-gold in color, round, and about 1 1/2 inches in diameter. They are the same lemons I found in Mexico and Guatemala and can also be considered the same as the Key lime of Florida. Because we do not have a readily available supply of these limes, I am using small yellow supermarket lemons.

1 3/4 cups salt
25 small yellow lemons, rinsed and patted dry with kitchen towels

1. Put 2 tablespoons of the salt in a large glass jar. Add the lemons (or limes if available to you) a few at a time and sprinkle salt over them. Do this with all the lemons and salt.
2. The jar must be placed in the sun each day for 1 month and shaken occasionally. The lemons will shrink a little and become soft and liquid will accumulate in the jar.

The lemons are ready to eat after 1 month. At this time, they can be sliced and eaten as a table chutney. Their tart, soft texture is an admirable accompaniment to Indian food.

Preserved lemons or limes are also included in several varieties of pickles. Salt is a preservative and the lemons do not need to be refrigerated. However, they must be covered.

Makes at least 2 quarts.

LIME PICKLE #1

 3 cups peanut oil
20 green Florida limes
 1 cup cider vinegar
 2 tablespoons ground mustard seed
 2 teaspoons ground fenugreek (see Glossary)
 2 tablespoons ground cuminseed
 2 tablespoons sugar
 1 tablespoon salt
 1 tablespoon turmeric
10 Preserved Lemons (page 92), quartered

1. Bring the oil to a boil in a wok or pan, then cool for 10 minutes. Pour half the oil into another pan.
2. Quarter the fresh limes and remove the seeds. Pour the vinegar over the fresh limes.
3. To the oil in the first pan add the mustard seed, fenugreek, cuminseed, sugar, salt, and turmeric and cook over low heat for 2 minutes. Mix well, always using a wooden spoon.
4. Add the fresh limes, drained, and cook over low heat for 5 minutes. Add the preserved lemons, the reserved vinegar, and the oil from the second pan and simmer for 15 minutes, or until the mixture is thick like jam. Remove from the heat.
   Cool completely. Transfer the pickle to 6 jars. Let mature for 1 week before using.

Makes about 1 quart.

LIME PICKLE #2

12 green Florida limes
2 tablespoons white vinegar (for rinsing)
2 tablespoons salt
1/2 pound fresh ginger, peeled
1/2 pound garlic, peeled
3/4 cup plus 2 tablespoons cider vinegar
3/4 cup peanut oil
1 cup sugar
1/2 teaspoon red chili powder
1/2 teaspoon cuminseed
5 small whole hot green chilis

1. Rinse the limes in the white vinegar. Quarter the limes and re-move the seeds.
2. In a food processor grind the ginger and garlic together with the 2 tablespoons cider vinegar and salt. Heat the oil slightly in a wok or pan and add the ginger-garlic paste. Add the sugar, chili powder, and cuminseed, mix well, and simmer for 2 min-utes.
3. Add the limes, chilis, and the 3/4 cup vinegar and stir-fry over low heat for 15 minutes. The mixture should thicken like jam. The oil will rise and cover the limes. Cool completely.

   Transfer the pickle to a glass jar and let mature, covered, for 1 week before tasting.

   Divide the pickle among 5 jars.

Makes about 1 quart.

LIME PICKLE #3

Local usage calls this lime pickle, although yellow lemons are used.

25 small yellow lemons, rinsed, patted dry, and quartered
1 cup salt
1/3 cup red chili powder
1 tablespoon turmeric
2 tablespoons ground fenugreek (see Glossary)
2 tablespoons ground yellow mustard seed
2 tablespoons fresh ginger, peeled and ground to a paste
2 tablespoons garlic, ground to a paste
3 cups peanut oil
2 cups cider vinegar

1. Toss the lemon pieces with the salt and set aside.
2. Put all the remaining ingredients in a pan and simmer over low heat for 5 minutes.
3. Add the salted lemon pieces and cook for 10 minutes. Remove the pan from the heat and cool completely.

   Bottle in glass jars. Let the pickle mature for 2–3 weeks before tasting.

Makes about 2 quarts.

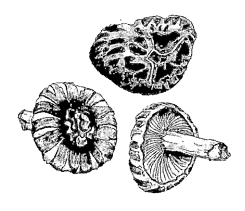

MANGO AMCHOOR

25 *large green, sour mangoes, peeled, quartered, and seeds discarded*
 4 *tablespoons salt*
10 *cloves garlic, peeled and sliced*
16 *whole cloves garlic, peeled*
 2 *inches fresh ginger, peeled and sliced*
 6 *tablespoons sugar*
 1 *cup cider vinegar*
 1 *heaping tablespoon yellow mustard seed, coarsely ground*
10 *large dried hot red chilis*
1/4 *teaspoon turmeric*
1/2 *cup mustard oil, slightly warmed*

1. Toss the chopped mangoes with the salt and store in a glass jar overnight. The next day, discard the liquid that has accumulated. Dry the mango pieces in one layer on a tray in the sun for 2 days. (The adventurous spirit will dry the mango pieces in a 200 degree oven for 24 hours.)
2. Mix the dried mangoes and all the remaining ingredients together in a large pan, bring the mixture just to a boil over moderate heat, and remove the pan from the heat. Cool completely.
3. Store, covered, in a glass or stone jar—do not use plastic—in a dark place to mature for 1 month before using.

Makes about 1 gallon.

NOTE: Mustard oil is available in any well-stocked Indian market.

M A H A S H A
Stuffed Mango Pickle

This is a light green pickle without a complicated mixture of spices.

10 *large hard, green, sour mangoes (10 pounds)*
 6 *tablespoons salt*
 3 *inches fresh ginger, peeled and sliced thin*
16 *cloves garlic, peeled and sliced thin*
 3 *tablespoons mustard seed, coarsely ground*
20 *small whole hot green chilis*
 1 *quart water*
1/2 *cup plus 3 tablespoons mustard oil*

1. Cut each mango three-fourths of the way open from the narrow to the thick end. Do *not* break open the 2 halves; the
   mango must remain intact. Sprinkle into the incision a liberal
   amount of salt. Put the mangoes in a glass or stone jar and set
   aside, covered, overnight.
2. By the next day the mangoes will have softened considerably.
   Carefully cut out and discard the seeds, but again, do not break
   apart the 2 halves. Place the mangoes on a tray and air-dry
   them for 4 hours at room temperature. Reserve the salty liquid.
3. Mix together the ginger, garlic, mustard seed, chilis, and the 3
   tablespoons mustard oil. Stuff each mango with about 1 tablespoon of the spice mixture and close the 2 sides of the mango
   together. Place in a glass or stone jar. Repeat with the remaining mangoes.
4. Mix the water with the reserved salty liquid. In a pan bring it
   to a boil, strain it through a metal strainer into a bowl, and let
   cool. Pour over the mangoes in the jar.
5. Slightly warm, then cool the 1/2 cup mustard oil. Pour it over
   the mangoes; it should completely immerse them. Let this
   pickle mature for 4–6 weeks in kitchen storage before using.

Makes about 2 quarts.

KASHMIR MANGO PICKLE

4 pounds hard, green, sour mangoes, peeled (about 4 large)
1 quart cider vinegar
12 ounces tamarind paste
2 pounds sugar
1/2 pound garlic, peeled
5 ounces salt
5 ounces yellow mustard seed, coarsely ground
3 ounces red chili powder
1/2 cup mustard oil, heated, then cooled

1. Halve the mangoes and cut out and discard the seeds. Cut up the pulp and in a food processor process it with 1/2 cup of the vinegar to a smooth paste.
2. Soak the tamarind paste in 1/2 cup of the vinegar, loosening it with your fingers. Squeeze the tamarind out through a piece of cheesecloth into a bowl and discard the seeds and fibres.
3. To the mango paste in the processor add the remaining vinegar together with the tamarind juice, sugar, garlic, salt, mustard seed, and chili powder. Process lightly but do not purée as there should be some texture. Transfer to a glass or stone jar. Pour the mustard oil over the pickle to cover it and protect it from contamination. Let the pickle mature for 2 months in kitchen storage before using.

Makes about 2 quarts.

MANGO PICKLE

12 *green, sour mangoes (5 pounds), rinsed and patted dry*
2 *tablespoons salt*
1/2 *pound fresh ginger, peeled and sliced*
1/2 *pound garlic, peeled and sliced*
1 1/2 *cups cider vinegar*
3 *tablespoons hot red chilis*
3 *tablespoons cuminseed*
1/2 *teaspoon pepper*
1/4 *teaspoon fenugreek powder (see Glossary)*
2 *tablespoons yellow mustard seed, ground*
1 *tablespoon turmeric*
2 *cups peanut oil*
1/3 *cup sugar*

1. Quarter the mangoes and discard the seeds. Toss well with the salt and place on a tray in the sun to air-dry for 1 day.
2. Grind the ginger and garlic in 1/2 cup of the vinegar to a relatively smooth paste in a food processor. Pound in a mortar with a pestle or grind in the processor the chilis, cuminseed, pepper, fenugreek powder, mustard seed, and turmeric.
3. Heat the oil slightly over low heat in a wok and add the ground and pounded ingredients and spices. Stir-fry for 1 minute and add the sugar, the remaining vinegar, and mangoes. Mix well. Simmer the pickle until the oil rises, about 20 to 30 minutes, stirring frequently to prevent burning. Remove from the heat and transfer to a glass or stone jar. Store for 1 week at room temperature before serving.

   Divide the pickle among 5 or 6 bottles. It may be served at this time, although like all pickles and chutneys the flavor is improved through maturation.

Makes about 1 quart.

HOT MANGO AND MUSTARD OIL PICKLE

This pickle must be allowed to mature before you taste it as it is not cooked and is too bitter if eaten earlier.

20 young small green mangoes (5 pounds), unpeeled
3/4 cup salt
2 tablespoons dried red chili flakes, crushed
1/4 cup coarsely ground mustard seed
1 teaspon fenugreek powder (see Glossary)
1/4 teaspoon turmeric
1/2 pound garlic, peeled and crushed to a paste
1 1/2 cups mustard oil, slightly warmed

1. Quarter the mangoes and discard the seeds. Toss well with the salt and let stand overnight at room temperature.
2. The next day remove the mango pieces, strain the liquid that accumulated, and in a pan boil them for 1 minute. Cool and reserve. Dry the mango pieces in the sun or in the air for 2 hours.
3. Mix the mango pieces with all the remaining ingredients. Stir in the reserved salted liquid.
4. Divide the pickle among 6 or 7 jars with tight covers. Pour mustard oil into each bottle, making sure it covers all the ingredients. Let the pickle mature in the sun or in kitchen storage for 2 months.

Makes about 2 quarts.

B R I N J A L   P I C K L E

The Hindi word *brinjal* has become the generic term for eggplant in India. I never even heard it referred to as eggplant.

6 *pounds fresh large firm* brinjal, *rinsed and dried*
1 *tablespoon salt*
2 *teaspoons turmeric*
2 *cups peanut oil*
1 *tablespoon ground cumin*
1/2 *pound fresh ginger, peeled and sliced*
1/2 *pound garlic, peeled and sliced*
2 *cups sugar*
2 *tablespoons paprika (for color)*
2 *cups cider vinegar*
20 *small whole hot green chilis*

1. Cut the *brinjal* into 1 1/2-inch cubes, toss with the salt and turmeric, and put on a tray to dry for an entire day. Drain the liquid that accumulates in a colander.
2. The next day, in a pan bring the oil to a boil over low heat. Cool for 15 minutes. Add the cumin, ginger, garlic, sugar, paprika, and vinegar and stir-fry over low heat for 10 minutes.
3. Add the *brinjal* and chilis and stir-fry continuously for 15 minutes. Do not mash or break up the *brinjal* pieces when cooking. The oil must cover the pickle; if it does not, then heat additional oil to add to the pan so that it will.

   Put the pickle in a glass or stone jar and allow it to mature for 1 week before bottling. It may be tasted at this time. Transfer to 5 or 6 bottles.

Makes about 2 quarts.

WILD PLUM PICKLE

Wild plums, as they are called in Calcutta, are collected in the hills, then turned into this spiced but not-too-sharp-with-chili pickle. It has a different taste from mango pickle and is popular even with those pickle aficionados. I suggest using in the United States the hard, sour Greengage plums as a substitute.

3 *pounds hard, green, sour plums*
1/2 *pound garlic, peeled and ground to a paste*
1/2 *pound fresh ginger, peeled and ground to a paste*
2–3 *tablespoons red chili powder, to taste*
2 *tablespoons black or yellow mustard seeds, ground*
1 *quart white vinegar*
3 *cups peanut oil*
1/2 *pound brown sugar*

1. Rinse and dry the plums. Cut them in half but do not remove the pits. Dry in the sun on a tray for 1 day.
2. In a food processor, grind the garlic and ginger pastes, the chili powder, and mustard seeds with 1/2 cup of the vinegar to a paste. Set aside.
3. Bring the oil in a pan to a boil. Remove from the heat and cool.
4. Add the spice paste to the oil and stir-fry it over moderate heat for 2 minutes. Add the plums, brown sugar, and the remaining vinegar. Cook, stirring to dissolve the sugar, until the oil rises, about 15 minutes.

   Cool. Divide the pickle among 5 or 6 bottles. Let stand 4 days to mature before tasting.

Makes 1 quart.

TOMATO KASUNDI, A PICKLE

1 pound dark brown sugar
1/2 cup golden raisins
1 1/2 cups cider vinegar
1 inch fresh ginger, peeled and sliced
10 cloves garlic, peeled and sliced
1 cup peanut oil
1 teaspoon ground cumin
1 teaspoon ground mustard seed
2 teaspoons red chili powder
2 teaspoons salt
1 teaspoon turmeric
4 pounds (8) ripe, firm tomatoes, quartered

1. Mix the sugar, raisins, and 1 cup of the vinegar together in a small pan and bring to a boil over low heat. Grind the ginger and garlic in 1/2 cup of the vinegar in a food processor and set aside.
2. Heat the oil in a large pan, remove from the heat, and cool for 10 minutes. Add the ginger/garlic paste, cumin, mustard seed, chili powder, salt, and turmeric and simmer over low heat for 5 minutes.
3. Add the tomatoes and raisin mixture and cook for 15–20 minutes, as the oil rises. Taste the pickle during the cooking process to adjust the sugar and salt in this sweet, sour, hot mixture. Cool completely.

   Transfer to 4 or 5 jars and let mature for 2 days before using.

Makes 1 quart.

How to Make Vinegar

Vinegar is home made from overripe fruit such as mangoes, peaches, plums, or other fruits of the season.

10 pounds overripe fruit
1 cup water
1/2 teaspoon acetic acid

Put all the ingredients in a stone crock, cover, and let it stand at room temperature for 2–3 weeks. Remember that temperatures in Calcutta during the days are hot and fermentation is rapid.

Gently squeeze the liquid from the fruit into a pan. The liquid is then boiled for 10 minutes, which kills the bacteria, cooled, and bottled. The finished product is a mild-flavored fruit vinegar. The fruit is discarded.

VARIATION

This method of vinegar-making is submitted for historical purposes: Jaggery is dark brown sugar. It and water are mixed together in a stone crock, then left to stand for 2 months. Every now and then, the mixture is stirred to dissolve the sugar. During this time the mixture is converted to a dark vinegar.

⚜ 4 ⚜

AN ARMENIAN CULINARY ODYSSEY

FOR THE Armenians, the road from Armenia to Calcutta was a long one: They left Yerevan, the capital city of the country in the Caucasus Mountains, sojourned in Julfa, a suburb of Isfahan in Persia, and finally established a small, albeit important, community in Calcutta in the early part of the seventeenth century. This would place the Armenians in what was not yet the city of Calcutta *before* Job Charnock arrived for the British East India Company in 1690. An Armenian tombstone confirms the date of their arrival.

The oldest Christian church in Calcutta, which is still in use, is the Armenian Holy Church of Nazareth. It was built in the burial ground and a number of the oldest tombs are in the floor of the church as well as the surrounding grounds. Some of the artifacts of this community are the monumental buildings, such as Gaulston Mansion, among many others, built on Park Street by Armenian architects and builders.

I have attempted to trace the sojourn of the Armenians via a culinary path, by first visiting the Armenian quarter in the Old City of Jerusalem on the hope of finding the classic dishes of the first traders who left Armenia for distant shores. It is arguably logical that the authentic culinary ideas would be in this ancient quarter. Some of these recipes are recorded in the following pages.

I was honored to be invited to the ancient Armenian quarter in the Old City of Jerusalem to observe, taste, and cook the classic dishes of that early Christian community. The kitchen I shared was at the top of an apartment building that overlooked the quarter and beyond to Jordan. I walked a circuitous route from the entrance to the quarter to the apartment. It was a thrilling and unbelievable experience to learn an ancient cultural manifestation in this historical setting.

Since Christianity came to Armenia in the fourth century A.D., one can assume that the early development of the cuisine began about 2,600 years ago and has continued until the present time in one form or another. Given the Armenians' tenacious attachment to their identity, why should the development of a cuisine be less intense than the implacable knowledge of their religion?

The recipes included here from the Old City are possibly the classic ones from Yerevan, the capital city of Armenia in the Caucasus and the first step in the movement of Armenian traders who moved to Julfa in Persia and thence the long trek to Calcutta.

The Armenians in Calcutta have developed their own menus, which are different from those they knew in Julfa, Persia, and even farther back in Yerevan. When a community moves from one region to another, whether it be benevolent or forced migration, the food consumed is altered. Different spices, seasonings, meats, and dairy products influence the daily choices, as does the respective dishes' popularity.

The Armenians in Calcutta do not, surprisingly, have any ethnic chicken recipes, except those that are part of the Indian menu. The Armenian meat of preference is mutton, or lamb as we know it. They also do not have fish recipes since their city of origin is Julfa, which is the Armenian suburb of Isfahan, Persia. This would not, on the other hand, eliminate fish or seafood in their diet if they chose to absorb the Indian menu.

In the early days in Calcutta—that is, in the seventeenth century and later—the Armenians used *ghee*, which they found in India, as a cooking medium. In the twentieth century, groundnut (peanut) oil replaced *ghee*.

As the Armenian recipes of Calcutta illustrate, the food of this ethnic subset is an amalgam of the ideas they brought with them from Persia and the ideas, spices, and seasoning they found in Calcutta. For example, kofta curry (beef ball curry) is absolutely Indian, made with curry powder, ginger, *garam masala*, coconut milk, and, naturally, the personal preference of the family who was transforming the dish into Armenian. *Khoo khoo* (mixed greens omelette) is much closer to their Persian roots, reflecting the many omelette combinations they brought with them to India. And so it goes. The culinary historian on the trail can trace the origin of a recipe or culinary habit, depending upon the knowledge and movements of the community. See Stuffed Grape Leaves (pg. 110) for a perfect example of this.

The Armenian Church, Calcutta

The Armenian food of Calcutta, with its wide range of ideas and flavors, will appeal to the adventurous temperament of American cooks and is presented here for its historical appeal as well as for its uniqueness as a cuisine in its own right.

NOTE: You will see the word Jerusalem in parentheses after the title of certain recipes that follow. It indicates that recipe's origin: The Armenians are widely dispersed. In order to connect them with the Calcutta group, I traveled to the Old City of Jerusalem, because Iran, as a destination, was not a possibility.

M I S A N D K H A S H O
Lamb and Vegetable Soup

This is one of the most popular of the Armenian soups, and it is also a one-course meal that can be prepared in two different ways.

1 pound whole lamb shank
6 cups water
1 teaspoon salt
2 medium potatoes, chopped (1 cup)
1 medium onion, chopped
1/2 cup dried white haricot beans, soaked in water overnight and drained
1/3 cup dried chick-peas, soaked in water overnight and drained
1 pound ripe fresh tomato or canned tomatoes, processed to a smooth paste

1. Put the lamb, water, and salt in a pan and bring the water to a boil over high heat. Remove the foam that accumulates on the surface. Cook for 15 minutes.
2. Add the potatoes, onion, beans, and chick-peas and cook, covered, over moderate heat until the meat is tender, about 1 1/2 hours. Add the tomato paste and cook for 10 minutes more.
3. Remove the lamb shank and remove the meat from the bone. Serve with the soup and vegetables. Or, strain the soup into another pan and serve it clear. Purée the meat and vegetables together, season with salt and pepper to taste, and serve the purée as a separate course. Serve both renditions warm.

Serves 4.

MIS PILAU
Rice, Lamb, and Vegetable Pilau

The basis for this pilau is Mis and Khasho, the renowned Armenian lamb and vegetable soup. First you prepare the soup. Then you cook rice in the soup broth. Then you combine the rice, meat, and vegetables and bake. Those several steps result in a one-dish combination that lends itself to easy and economical family dining.

1 recipe Mis and Khasho (page 108), lamb removed from the shank and cubed
2 tablespoons corn or peanut oil
2 cups basmati rice, well rinsed, soaked in water 1/2 hour, and drained

1. Heat the oil in a pan, add the rice, and stir-fry it for 2 minutes to lightly brown. Add the lamb broth, bring to a boil, cover the pan, and cook over low heat until all the liquid has been absorbed, about 12 minutes.
2. Scoop out a well in the rice and add the cubed lamb and all the vegetables, then cover with the rice. Bake, covered, in a preheated 350 degree oven for 15 minutes. Before serving, toss the ingredients together to combine and serve warm.

Serves 4.

SARMA
(JERUSALEM)
Stuffed Grape Leaves

A number of cultures stuff grape leaves. The idea is a good one since the flexible grape leaf can easily be turned into an envelope. Two stuffings, both vegetarian and well seasoned, follow. The choice is yours.

VEGETARIAN STUFFING #1
    2 cups chopped onions (about 4 medium)
    1 teaspoon salt
 1/3 cup olive oil
    1 medium sweet green pepper, seeded and chopped
 1/2 sweet red pepper, seeded and chopped
    1 cup chopped ripe tomato
    1 tablespoon tomato paste
 1/4 teaspoon white pepper
 1/2 teaspoon allspice
    1 cup rice, well rinsed
    1 cup water
    3 scallions, sliced thin
 1/3 cup chopped parsley
    1 pound jarred grape leaves, rinsed and stems removed
    3 cups water
 1/4 cup olive oil
      Juice of 2 lemons

1. Put the onions in a skillet, add the salt, and stir-fry over low heat for 3 minutes. Pour in the olive oil and cook until golden. Add the sweet peppers, tomato, tomato paste, pepper, and allspice and mix well.
2. Add the rice and 1/2 cup of the water. Cook until boiling and add the remaining water, simmering the mixture for 15 minutes. (The rice will be only partially cooked.) Remove the skillet from the heat and cool. Stir in the scallions and parsley.
3. Take 1 heaping tablespoon of the rice mixture and put it on a

grape leaf on the end nearest you. Roll the leaf firmly over the rice but allow space for expansion; tuck in the sides. A stuffed leaf should be about 3 inches long and 3/4 inch thick. Arrange the stuffed leaves, seam side down, in a pan and pour over them the water, oil, and lemon juice.

Bring the liquid to a boil, cover the pan, and cook over low heat for 45 minutes to tenderize the leaves. Cool and refrigerate.

Serve cold or at room temperature.

Makes about 40.

Here is another stuffing, without tomato, but enriched with pine nuts and currants.

VEGETARIAN STUFFING #2

6 cups thinly sliced onions
1/2 cup olive oil
1 cup rice, well rinsed
1/2 cup pine nuts
2 tablespoons dried currants
2 teaspoons chopped fresh or dried dill
1/2 teaspoon salt
1/4 teaspoon pepper
1 cup water (for cooking)

1. Stir-fry the onions in the olive oil in a skillet over low heat until golden, about 5 minutes. Add the rice, pine nuts, currants, dill, salt, and pepper and stir-fry for 5 minutes more. Cool.
2. Take 1 heaping tablespoon of the stuffing and put it on a grape leaf. Roll the leaves as directed above, then layer them, seam side down, in a pan. Add 1 cup water and place a plate over the leaves to weight them down. Bring the water to a boil, then cook over low heat for 45 minutes. Should the water evaporate before the end of the cooking time, add another 1/4 cup water. Cool and refrigerate. Serve cold or at room temperature.

Makes about 40.

Here is an assortment of different vegetables that can be stuffed, variations on the same theme. They can be eaten warm or cold.

- Lettuce leaves, softened 1 minute in boiling water
- Small eggplant, 6 to a pound, scooped out
- Small tomatoes, 5 or 6 to a pound, scooped out
- Kirby cucumbers, 3 inches long, peeled
- Bitter melon, cook separately from other vegetables on account of distinctive bitter flavor. Cut a 3-inch slit in the center of each melon; squeeze the ends toward each other, and scoop out the interior seeds and loose pulp. Stuff as other vegetables, stack in a pan, cover stack with a plate, add 1/2 cup water, and cook over low heat for 1/2 hour.

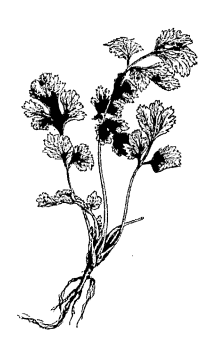

KHALAMA DOLMA
Stuffed Cabbage Rolls

Armenians enjoy stuffing vegetables. These cabbage rolls are one of several styles they make, well seasoned and cooked without oil. There is a touch of India here with the curry powder, as well as of the Middle East, where the stuffing of vegetables is a fine art.

A 2-pound head cabbage
1/2 pound beef steak, sliced
  1 small onion, sliced (1/3 cup)
  3 cloves garlic, sliced
1/2 inch fresh ginger, chopped
1/4 cup chopped fresh coriander (Chinese parsley), mint, and parsley, combined
1/8 teaspoon fenugreek powder (see Glossary)
1/3 cup rice, rinsed well
  1 tablespoon ghee *(clarified butter) or butter, melted*
  2 tablespoons golden raisins
  1 teaspoon curry powder
  1 teaspoon salt
  1 large ripe tomato
10 dried pitted prunes
1/2 cup water

1. Scoop out 1 inch of the core of the cabbage. Put the head of cabbage into a pan of boiling water to cover, let soak for 2 minutes, turn it over, then remove from the pan. Pull off as many leaves as you can that slip off easily. Blanch the head as many times as necessary in order to remove 20 leaves. Set aside.
3. In a food processor grind together the beef, onion, garlic, ginger, and herbs until coarse in texture. Mix in by hand the fenugreek, rice, *ghee*, raisins, curry powder, and salt.
4. Spread 1 cabbage leaf out. Place 1 heaping tablespoon of the beef mixture in the center, fold over the right and left sides, and roll up into a cylinder 3 inches long and 1 inch wide. Make

cabbage rolls with the remaining stuffing and leaves in the same manner.

5. Place all the rolls in concentric circles in a pan. Cover with tomato slices and 10 prunes. Add another layer of cabbage rolls, and top with a layer of tomatoes and then prunes. Try for 2 layers, using all the prunes. Pour the water over all. Place a flat plate on the rolls to hold them down. Cover the pan and cook over low heat for 1/2 hour. Serve warm with bread.

Makes 20 rolls.

DOLMA
(JERUSALEM)
Stuffed Eggplant or Zucchini Squash

Stuffings for both grape leaves and assorted vegetables are interchangeable. Several kinds of vegetarian or meat stuffings are appropriate and personal preference should be the guide.

8 *small eggplant or 8 small squash (2 pounds)*
A vegetarian stuffing for Sarma (pages 110, 111)
3 *cups water*
1/4 *cup olive oil*
Juice of 1 lemon

Scoop out the vegetables with a metal scooper, discarding the pulp and leaving a shell on each vegetable about 1/4 inch thick. Stuff the shells firmly but not too tightly with the vegetarian stuffing of choice. Fit the vegetables into a pan and pour in the water, oil, and lemon juice. Bring the liquid to a boil, cover the pan, then simmer over low heat for 45 minutes. Serve hot.

Serves 4 to 6.

MEAT STUFFING FOR DOLMA OR SARMA

1/2 *pound ground lamb or beef*
1 *cup rice, well rinsed*
2 *ripe fresh tomatoes or canned tomatoes, chopped (1 cup)*
1 *medium onion, chopped (1/2 cup)*
1/4 *cup chopped parsley*
2 *tablespoons tomato paste*
1/4 *teaspoon salt*
1/4 *teaspoon pepper*
1/4 *teaspoon allspice*

Mix all the ingredients together, except the water, to prepare the stuffing. Stuff the hollowed-out vegetables (or grape leaves) and arrange them in a pan with only 3 cups water. (Do not add lemon juice or oil.) Bring the liquid to a boil, cover the pan, and reduce the heat to low. Simmer for 45 minutes. Serve hot.

Serves 4 to 6.

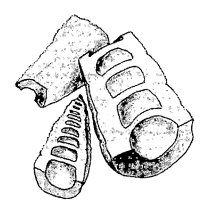

M A N T I
(JERUSALEM)
Miniature Stuffed Packets

This is one of the finest of all Armenian dishes and glorifies the cuisine. It is a time-consuming preparation that is served on Sunday for family dining and where family members are able to contribute filling the hundreds of packets sometimes called boats or canoes. It is recommended that family and friends be recruited when planning to make *manti*. Halving the recipe is perfectly acceptable and makes the experience less daunting, while it provides the experience of this wonderful dish.

THE DOUGH
- 6 *cups flour*
- 2 *large eggs*
- 1/8 *teaspoon salt*
- *About 1 cup water*

THE FILLING
- 2 *pounds ground lamb*
- 2 *medium onions, chopped (3/4 cup)*
- 1/2 *cup chopped parsley*
- 1 *teaspoon black pepper*
- 1 *teaspoon allspice*
- 1/2 *teaspoon paprika*
- 2 *cups hot chicken or beef broth*

1. Make the dough: Mix the flour, eggs, and salt together, adding enough of the water to form a soft dough. Make a long roll of the dough and divide it into 10 equal pieces.
2. Make the filling: Mix everything together well. Set aside.
3. Take 1 piece of the dough and cut it in half. Roll out each half to a thin strip 3 inches wide and as long as you can. (The strip should be almost paper thin.) Cut the strips into 1- to 1 1/4-inch squares.
2. Take 1/2 teaspoon of the meat filling, put it in the center of the square, and fold it up to the center. Pinch both ends closed to

the right and left, making a canoe or boat shape. A bit of meat will be visible emerging from the center. This is the miniature packet. Make packets in the same manner with the remaining ingredients.

4. Put all the packets side by side, meat side up, in round or rectangular metal baking dishes, well rubbed with butter or margarine. Arrange in circles if the dish is round (it was when I was learning this recipe in the Armenian Convent) or rectangles if the dish is rectangular. The packets should be close enough together to touch.

5. Bake in a preheated 350 degree oven for 20 minutes. The packets turn light brown with crisp edges. Remove the baking dishes from the oven and pour the hot broth over all. It will be absorbed by the *manti* and, in fact, tenderizes them. Serve hot, with a yoghurt side dish as follows: Mix 1 cup yoghurt and 2 cloves garlic, crushed through the press. Serve the sauce at room temperature spread over the *manti*.

Makes 20 packets.

PANIR
Armenian Cheese

During my early days in Calcutta, the chalk-white buffalo's milk and cream was thick and rich, not watered down—a common ploy of the milkman—and readily available. The passage of years has made the milk a little difficult to find. So, prepare this cheese with whole cow's milk instead.

1 quart buffalo's milk (or substitute whole cow's milk)
2 powdered rennet tablets or 1 teaspoon rennet liquid
  Coarse salt

1. Warm the milk to "blood heat" (98.6 F. or 37 C. degrees). Remove from the heat and dissolve the rennet in 1/4 cup of the warm milk. Add the rennet mixture back to the balance of the milk and stir to combine.
2. Cover the pan and let stand until the milk is firm. (This could be about 15 minutes.) Transfer the milk to the refrigerator and let cool completely.
3. Pour the milk into a cloth bag or fine kitchen towel with the ends tied together. Put the bag on a tilted board and let it drain for about 1 hour. This should be sufficient to firm up the cheese.
4. Cut the cheese into pieces, 3 by 1 inch each. Sprinkle with the coarse salt, arrange in a jar, and store in the refrigerator. To serve, rinse off the salt and eat with bread or toast.

Makes about 1/4 pound.

BIZARI HATHS
Bazaar Bread

This is the daily Armenian flat bread, with little or no leavening. There was a time when this bread could be purchased at the bazaar bakery, but now that the community has dwindled to a handful of families, the bread is prepared at home.

3 1/2–4 cups flour
    1 egg, beaten
  1/2 teaspoon sugar
  1/4 teaspoon salt
    1 tablespoon ghee (clarified butter) or butter, melted
  2–3 tablespoons cold water
      A good pinch of baking powder
      Oil for the baking tray

1. Mix all the ingredients together, except the oil, to form a firm but flexible dough. (Adjust the amounts of flour and water, as needed.) Let stand, covered, at room temperature for 1 hour.
2. Divide the dough into 6 equal pieces. Roll each piece into a 6-inch round.
3. Lightly oil a baking tray. Put the loaves in one layer on the tray and bake in a preheated 375 degree oven for about 15 minutes, or until colored a light brown. Serve warm, with butter, cheese, or Mis and Khasho, puréed (page 108).

Makes 6 round flat breads.

KHOO KHOO
Mixed Greens Omelette

The Persians have many omelette combinations, which they call *khoo khoo*. Since the Armenians in the Calcutta community came from Isfahan in Persia, it is logical to assume that they brought their omelette recipes with them.

This is an omelette for all seasons, but the Armenians especially prepare this on Christmas Eve, for the Easter evening dinner, and other celebrations.

3 *spring onions (scallions), chopped fine*
1 *small onion, chopped (1/3 cup)*
1/2 *cup loosely packed spinach, chopped fine*
1/2 *teaspoon salt*
4 *eggs, beaten until foamy*
1/2 *teaspoon curry powder*
1 *teaspoon flour*
Pinch of baking powder (optional)
2 *tablespoons* ghee *(clarified butter) or peanut oil*

1. Mix the spring onions, onion, spinach, and salt together and let stand 1/2 hour. Squeeze out the liquid.
2. Mix together the eggs, greens, curry powder, flour, and baking powder, if used, until well combined.
3. Heat the *ghee* or oil in a skillet over moderate heat. Add the egg mixture and cook for 5 minutes. Turn the omelette over carefully and cook 2 minutes more. Serve this 1-inch-thick omelette warm.

Serves 4.

KHUFTA
Beef and Vegetable Cutlet

Khufta (sometimes *kofta*, as in the curry recipe on page 124) are ground meat dishes that can become barbecues, fried patties, or, in this case, Armenian style, cutlets of ground beef, vegetables, and an assortment of spices and seasonings.

 1 pound ground beef or lamb
1/2 pound onion, chopped
1/2 pound potato, peeled and chopped
 2 teaspoons each of chopped fresh mint, fresh coriander, and flat-leaf parsley, combined
1/2 inch fresh ginger, chopped
 1 clove garlic, chopped
 1 hot green chili, chopped (about 1 tablespoon)
 1 teaspoon curry powder
 1 egg, beaten
1/2 teaspoon salt
 2 tablespoons flour
1/4 cup oil for pan-frying

1. Chop the beef, onion, potato, herbs, ginger, garlic, and chili, but not too fine. Add the curry powder, egg, salt, and flour and mix well. Let stand 1/2 hour.
2. Heat the oil in a skillet. Take 2 heaping tablespoons of the meat mixture, flatten slightly to about 3/8 inch thick, and brown on both sides in the oil. Drain briefly on paper towels. Shape cutlets and cook them in the same manner with the remaining mixture. Serve warm with bread.

Makes 15 cutlets.

4 medium potatoes (3/4 pound)

1 recipe Khufta

1/2 pound ripe tomatoes (2), sliced 1/4 inch thick

1/4 cup corn or peanut oil

1. Peel and slice the potatoes into rounds 1/4 inch thick. Soak in water with 1 teaspoon salt added for 15 minutes. Drain and pat dry.
2. Heat the oil in an ovenproof pan and brown the potatoes on both sides over moderate heat for 5 minutes. Set aside.
3. Fry the cutlets in a skillet for about 5 minutes. Add the cutlets to the pan. Spread the potatoes over the cutlets and the tomatoes over the potatoes. Cover the pan and bake in a preheated 350 degree oven for 15–20 minutes. Serve warm.

Serves 6 or more.

KOFTA CURRY
Beef Ball Curry

This is a typical Armenian curry with Indian overtones that includes onion, ginger, garlic, and curry powder, all blended together with rich coconut milk. There are several ways to handle cooking the meat balls: One is to add them to the sauce uncooked; the other way, which I personally prefer, is to place them on an oiled baking sheet and bake them in a 350 degree oven for 10 minutes. Then add them to the sauce. If precooked, they don't disintegrate thanks to the crust that forms when they are lightly baked.

THE KOFTA

   1 pound ground beef

   1 medium onion, finely chopped (1/2 cup)

1/2 teaspoon curry powder

1/2 teaspoon salt, or to taste

1/2 pound white bread, crusts removed, soaked in water, and squeezed out

THE SAUCE

   2 tablespoons peanut oil

   1 medium onion, finely chopped (1/2 cup)

   3 cloves garlic, finely chopped

   1 inch fresh ginger, peeled and finely chopped

1/2 teaspoon curry powder

1/2 cup water

   4 small potatoes (1/2 pound), peeled and cut into 4 pieces each

1/2 cup rich coconut milk

1/4 teaspoon garam masala *(see Glossary)*

1. Make the *kofta:* Mix the beef, the onion, curry powder, salt, and bread together well and shape into meat balls, each 1 1/2 inches in diameter.

2. Make the sauce: Heat the oil in a pan, add the onion, and stir-fry over moderate heat until light brown, about 3 or 4 minutes. Add the garlic, ginger, and curry powder and stir-fry 2 minutes, adding 1 teaspoon of the water to moisten.

3. Add the potatoes and remaining water and cook, covered, over

low heat for 10 minutes. Add the coconut milk, *garam masala*, and the beef balls. Cook, covered, for 15 minutes, or until the potatoes are soft and the beef balls are cooked through. The sauce will have thickened. Serve warm with Kidgeree Pilau (page 132). Since this curry is not strongly spiced, you may wish to serve it with hot Indian chutneys and pickles.

Serves 4 or 5.

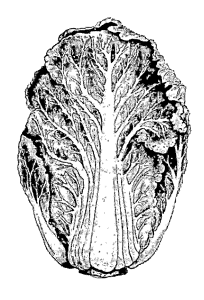

PHARING PILAU
Bulgur and Beef Bake

> The Armenian food of Calcutta has an assortment of unconventional
> combinations that depart from the classic ideas of Indian cooking. Bul-
> gur, which is cracked wheat fragments, is a specialty of the Middle East,
> yet it has found its way to Calcutta. Perhaps this can be explained by re-
> membering that the Armenian community originated in Julfa, a suburb
> of the ancient city of Isfahan, Iran.

THE BEEF
    2 *tablespoons corn or peanut oil*
    1 *pound beef chuck, cut into 2-inch cubes*
    2 *small whole onions*
    3 *cups water*
    1/2 *teaspoon salt*
    1 *teaspoon curry powder*

THE *BULGUR*
    1/4 *cup oil*
    1 *large onion, chopped (1 cup)*
    2 *cups coarse bulgur*
    1/2 *teaspoon* garam masala *(see Glossary)*
    1/2 *teaspoon salt*
       Reserved broth from the beef preparation, plus enough water to total
       4 cups
    1 *tablespoon sugar*
    2 *tablespoons water*

1. Make the beef: Heat the oil in a pan and brown the beef and
   onions over moderate heat for 5 minutes. Add the water, salt,
   and curry powder and cook, covered, until the beef is tender,
   about 40 minutes. Remove all the broth, measure it, and reserve.
2. Heat the oil in a pan and brown the onion over moderate heat
   for 2 minutes. Add the bulgur and stir constantly until the
   color changes, about 5 minutes.

3. Sprinkle the *garam masala* and salt over all and add the reserved broth and water mixture. Cover and cook until the water is absorbed and the grains of bulgur separate when fluffed up.
4. In a skillet caramelize the sugar. Add the water to dissolve it.
5. Make a well in the bulgur, add the meat, then cover it with the bulgur. Pour the melted caramelized sugar over the top. Cover the pan and bake in a preheated 350 degree oven for 20 minutes. Serve warm with bread.

Serves 6.

MISOV KOOFTE
(JERUSALEM)
Armenian Meat Patties

THE PATTIES
> 2 *pounds ground lamb as prepared for Manti (page 117)*
> 2 *cloves garlic, crushed through a garlic press*
> 1/4 *cup corn oil for pan-frying*

THE VEGETABLES
> 3 *medium fresh tomatoes, sliced (1 1/2 cups), or canned*
> 1 *sweet green pepper, seeded and cut into long slices*
> 1 *tablespoon tomato paste dissolved in 1/2 cup water*
> 1/4 *teaspoon salt*

1. Make the patties: Mix the lamb and garlic together. Moisten your hands with cold water, then take 1 tablespoon of the meat mixture and make a round ball. Flatten the ball out slightly to 1 1/2 inches in diameter and about 3/8 inch thick.
2. Heat the oil in a skillet and fry the patties over moderate heat for 2–3 minutes, or to the desired degree of doneness. Drain on paper towels.
3. Prepare the vegetables: Using the same skillet as the *koofte*, and it should still be lightly oiled, stir-fry the tomatoes and pepper with the tomato paste and salt over moderate heat for 2 minutes.
4. Arrange the tomatoes over the bottom of a Pyrex or metal baking dish, top with the green pepper strips. Arrange the *koofte* over the peppers and pour any liquid remaining in the skillet over all. Bake in a preheated 350 degree oven for 1/2 hour. Serve warm with potato purée or rice, both of them traditional favorites.

Makes 20 patties.

LULA KEBOB
Minced Lamb Barbecue

A kebob is meat and/or vegetables barbecued on a short metal skewer. In the home, the skewers are grilled over a *chula*, which is a metal milk pail that has been modified with a grill. Coal or charcoal are the cooking fuels of choice and during the winter months in Calcutta (October to March) the pollution from a million or more of these burning all day to heat or cook is thick enough to block out the sky.

    2 pounds ground lamb
    1 pound onions, chopped, the liquid squeezed out through a cloth
    2 cloves garlic, ground to a paste
  1/2 inch fresh ginger, peeled and ground to a paste
    1 teaspoon ground cumin
    1 teaspoon salt, or to taste
  3/4 teaspoon garam masala (see Glossary)
1/2–1 teaspoon hot red chili powder
  1/2 teaspoon turmeric
  1/4 teaspoon ground cinnamon

1. Mix all the ingredients together by hand or briefly in a food processor.
2. Select 12 skewers, each with a flat blade so that the meat mixture will adhere firmly to it. Put about 2 heaping tablespoons of the meat mixture on each skewer to form a 5-inch round kabob with 1/4-inch meat all around. Grill over charcoal or in a broiler for about 2 minutes on each side, which is sufficient to cook the kabob. Serve warm with bread, salad, chutney, and perhaps a side dish of fresh hot green chilis.

Makes about 12 kebobs.

M U S A M B I
Meat and Eggplant Bake

This dish is not at all Indian in character as it does not contain the dynamic spicing of India. It does have a strong hint of Persian influence, however, and makes a family-style one-dish meal with lots of flavor and dimension but very little meat. Besides being called *musambi*, it is also known as *dampkbkot*.

1 pound boneless beef or lamb, cut into 2-inch cubes
2 cups water
2 teaspoon salts
8–10 small eggplant (2 pounds), peeled
1/4 cup corn or peanut oil, plus 1 tablespoon
1/2 pound small whole pickling onions, peeled
4 small whole potatoes, 1/2 pound, peeled
1 pound fresh tomatoes (3), sliced
1 teaspoon curry powder
1 tablespoon sugar
3 tablespoons cider vinegar

1. In a pan cook the beef in the water with 1 teaspoon of the salt over moderate heat, covered, until tender, about 45 minutes.
2. Sprinkle the eggplant with the remaining 1 teaspoon salt and let stand 1/2 hour. Rinse under cold water and pat dry.
3. Heat the 1/4 cup oil in a skillet and in separate batches brown the eggplant, onions, and potatoes, removing each to a plate. Then lightly brown the meat.
4. Put the 1 tablespoon oil in a rectangular baking dish. Arrange the meat on the bottom, top with the potatoes, then the onions, and finally the eggplant. Cover the layer of eggplant with the tomatoes and sprinkle them with the curry powder. Then sprinkle with the sugar and vinegar. Bake in a preheated 350 degree oven for 1/2 hour. Serve warm.

Serves 6 or more.

Pista Badam Pilau
Almond and Pistachio Rice

This is a rich pilau that can be eaten alone, but is generally served with any kind of curry.

1 cup rice, rinsed in cold water and drained
2 tablespoons peanut oil
1 medium onion, coarsely chopped (1/2 cup)
2 tablespoons golden raisins
1 3/4 cups water
1/4 teaspoon salt, or to taste
2 tablespoons blanched almonds, halved lengthwise
2 tablespoons pistachio nuts, halved

1. Soak the rice in water for 1/2 hour. Drain.
2. Heat the oil in an ovenproof pan, add the onion, and stir-fry until the pieces are light brown but the edges are dark. Add the rice and stir until it changes color, about 2 minutes.
3. Add the raisins, water, and salt and cook over low heat, covered, for 10 minutes. Stir the almonds and pistachio nuts into the rice. Cover the pan and bake in a preheated 350 degree oven for 15 minutes. Serve warm.

Serves 4.

KIDGEREE PILAU
Rice and Red Lentils

The rice here is enriched with red lentils, also known as Egyptian lentils, which are one of the many varieties found in India. They provide not only protein but also flavor. Kidgeree is usually served with *kofta* (meat ball) curry.

2 cups rice, rinsed in cold water and drained
1 cup red lentils (Egyptian)
3 tablespoons oil
1/4 teaspoon turmeric
4 cups water
1/2 teaspoon salt

1. Soak the rice in cold water for 1/2 hour. Drain. Soak the lentils in water overnight. Drain.
2. Heat the oil in a pan, add the rice and turmeric, and stir-fry over moderate heat for 3–4 minutes to brown the rice lightly. Add the water and salt, cover the pan, and cook over low heat for 10 minutes, or until the rice has absorbed the water.
3. Make a well in the rice, pour in the lentils, then cover them with the rice. Cover the pan and cook over very low heat for 15–20 minutes. (This should be sufficient to soften the lentils.) Stir the rice and lentils together to combine and turn out onto a serving platter. Serve warm with Kofta Curry (page 124).

Serves 4–6.

SAMITH PILAU
Rice with Dill

The Armenian rice dishes of Calcutta owe an allegiance to the classic methods of rice preparation in Persia. This recipe is a good example, one where rice is glorified with a fresh herb.

> 2 cups rice, rinsed in cold water and drained
> 3 tablespoons peanut oil
> 3 1/2 cups boiling water
> 1/2 cup finely chopped fresh dill
> 1/2 teaspoon salt

1. Soak the rice in water for 1/2 hour. Drain.
2. Heat the oil in a pan, add the rice, and stir-fry it over moderate heat for 3 minutes. Add the water, dill, and salt, stir to mix, cover the pan, and cook over low heat for 15 minutes. Remove from the heat and let stand, covered, for 10 minutes before serving. Serve warm.

Serves 6.

NOTE: Fresh or frozen green peas are sometimes included in this green pilau. If used, add 1/2 cup of them at the same time as you do the water.

GREEN PEA PILAU

This pilau is prepared in the same way as Rice with Dill (page 133), except that the dill is omitted and peas are added.

2 cups rice, rinsed in cold water and drained
2 tablespoons peanut oil
3 1/2 cups boiling water
1/2 teaspoon salt
1 cup fresh or frozen green peas

1. Soak the rice in water for 1/2 hour. Drain.
2. Heat the oil in a pan, add the rice, and stir-fry it for 3 minutes over low heat, which will lightly brown it. Add the water, salt, and green peas, bring the water to a boil, cover the pan, and cook for 15 minutes. Remove the pan from the heat, stir the rice and peas together, cover again, and let stand 10 minutes before serving. Serve warm.

Serves 6.

POTATO PILAU

4 small potatoes (1 pound), peeled and cut into rounds 1/4 inch thick
1/4 cup peanut oil
1 recipe Green Pea Pilau (page 134), made without the peas

1. Soak the potatoes in water with 1 teaspoon salt added for 15 minutes. Drain well and dry on kitchen towels.
2. Heat the oil in a pan and lightly brown the potatoes over moderate heat for 5 minutes. (This will also soften them.) Arrange the potatoes in the bottom of a baking pan. Top with the green pea pilau. Cover the pan and bake in a preheated 350 degree oven for 15 minutes. Serve warm with any kind of Armenian or Indian curry.

Serves 6.

Naan Roti Pilau

Naan *roti* is a spongy handmade bread with yeast leavening that is baked in a tandoor. Naan *roti* is traditional in places like India, Pakistan, and Afghanistan. The round pita breads found in Middle East bakeries can be substituted here.

1 *baked* naan roti
3 *tablespoons peanut oil*
1 *recipe Green Pea Pilau (page 134)*

Heat the oil in a pan, add the *naan roti,* and brown it for 2 minutes on each side. Cover the *roti* with the green pea pilau and bake it, covered, in a preheated 350 degree oven for 15 minutes. Serve warm.

Serves 6.

KHOO KHOO PILAU
Spinach (or Green Leaf) Pilau

A pilau is a classic method of cooking rice by first browning it in oil and then adding water and seasonings. Here is an Armenian-style green pilau.

Any kind of green leaf may be used in this pilau. The Armenians use the word *saag*, which refers to a spinach-like leaf grown in Bengal. Spinach works well and so does the green leaf of Swiss chard.

> 2 cups rice, rinsed in cold water and drained
> 3 tablespoons peanut oil
> 1/2 cup finely chopped spinach
> 3 1/2 cups water
> 1/2 teaspoon salt

1. Soak the rice in water for 1/2 hour. Drain.
2. Heat the oil in a pan, add the rice and spinach, and stir-fry over moderate heat for about 3 minutes to brown the rice lightly. Add the water and salt and bring to a boil. Reduce the heat to low, cover the pan, and cook for 12 minutes. (The rice will absorb the water.) Stir once or twice toward the end of the cooking time. Remove the pan from the heat and let it stand, covered, for 10 minutes more before serving. Serve warm with *Khoo Khoo* (page 121).

Serves 4–6.

KOFTA PISH PASH
Soft Rice and Meat Balls

I am not certain about the origin of the expression, "pish pash" as it applies to this dish. During my Calcutta years, pish pash meant combining leftover meat, usually roast lamb, cut into cubes, with an equal amount of cooked cubed potatoes, curry spices, onion, and garlic, then stir-frying it together until brown. It was very delicious and, to me, exotic. This *kofta pish pash* is entirely different and Armenian.

THE MEAT BALLS

    1 *pound ground beef*
    1 *medium onion, chopped (1/2 cup)*
    2 *cloves garlic, sliced*
    1 *inch fresh ginger, peeled and chopped*
    2 *tablespoons chopped fresh coriander (Chinese parsley)*
    1 *tablespoon chopped fresh mint*
  1/4 *teaspoon fenugreek powder (see Glossary)*
1 or 2 *hot green chilis, to taste, sliced*
  1/2 *teaspoon salt*
  1/2 *teaspoon curry powder*
    3 *tablespoons peanut oil*
    6 *cups water*
  1/4 *teaspoon salt*

THE SOFT RICE

    1 *cup rice, rinsed*
  1/4 *cup chopped fresh coriander (Chinese parsley)*

1. Make the meat balls: Mix everything together either by hand or preferably in a processor to a smooth consistency. With your hands, shape into meat balls, each about 2 inches in diameter. Makes 6 or 7.
2. Heat the oil in a pan, add the water and salt, and bring to a boil over moderate heat. Add the meat balls, one at a time, and cook them until they float, about 5 minutes.
3. Add the rice and cook for 10 minutes. Stir in the coriander and simmer over low heat for 10–15 minutes more to ensure that the rice is soft. Serve warm.

Serves 4.

Whole wheat kernels may be used instead of rice. They must first be soaked overnight in water and drained before using. Add the soaked wheat kernels to the boiling water with 1 tablespoon tomato purée and proceed as directed above for rice pish pash.

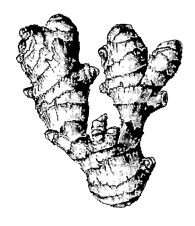

SHELA PILAU
(PISH PASH)
Soft Rice with Chicken

This is a soothing chicken porridge, a simple dish for those days when heavy and complicated food is not wanted. A Calcutta friend told me that when members of his family were feeling out of sorts *shela pilau* was served to revive flagging spirits.

A 3-pound chicken, cut into 8 pieces, loose skin and fat discarded
6 *cups water*
1 *teaspoon salt*
2 *cups rice, well rinsed in cold water and drained*
2 *tablespoons butter or peanut oil*
2 *tablespoons chopped fresh coriander (Chinese parsley)*

1. In a large pot cook the chicken in the water with the salt over moderate heat for 15 minutes. Remove and discard the foam as it rises.
2. Add the rice, butter or oil, and coriander, cover the pot, and cook until the rice is soft, about 20 to 25 minutes. The chicken will also become tender during this time. Serve warm.

Serves 8.

H A T I C
Bean Cook for Lent

During Lent, the period of penitence and self-denial, the Armenians, who are Christian, do not eat rich foods like meat and certain oils that are also forbidden. Services are held in their remarkable and ancient church in old Calcutta.

This is a special Lenten dish, customarily served with Pickled Onions (page 142).

1 cup dried white haricot beans
1 cup dried chick-peas
2 cups black lentils (masoor dal, *available at Indian markets*)
1 cup whole wheat kernels
8 cups water
3 medium onions, chopped (1 1/2 cups)
3 whole dried hot red chilis
1 teaspoon salt, or to taste

1. Soak the beans, peas, lentils, and wheat kernels separately in water to cover overnight. Drain.
2. Put the 8 cups water, drained bean mixture, and all the remaining ingredients in a large pan and bring the water to a boil. Cook over moderate/low heat for 1 to 1 1/2 hours, or until all the ingredients are soft. Serve warm with pickled onions.

Serves 8.

CATZAKHIE SOKH
Pickled Onions

Pickled onions make a handy kind of chutney or side dish with curry dinners or with any of the ethnic regional foods of India. They are the traditional accompaniment to the Lenten bean dish called Hatic (page 141).

1 cup white or cider vinegar
1 teaspoon sugar
1 teaspoon salt
1 pound small white pickling onions, peeled
3 whole hot green chilis

1. Put the vinegar, sugar, and salt in a pan and bring to a boil over moderate heat. Remove and cool.
2. Put the onions and chilis in a jar and pour over them the vinegar solution. Cover the jar and let stand at room temperature for 4 days before using. After opening, refrigerate, tightly covered.

Makes 3 cups.

JAJIK
(JERUSALEM)
Yoghurt Salad

This is a simple, traditional, cooling summer salad.

1 cup yoghurt
1/2 cup cubed cucumber (1/4-inch pieces)
1 clove garlic, crushed through a garlic press
1/2 teaspoon dried mint, or 2 teaspoons chopped fresh mint
1/8 teaspoon salt

Mix all the ingredients together and refrigerate until serving time. Serve cold.

Serves 4.

⁓ 5 ⁓
ANGLO-INDIAN COOKING:
THE BENGAL CLUB

NOSTALGIA MAKES the world go round.

The Bengal Club at 1/1 Russell Street in the center of Calcutta is the last bastion of the British Empire and an oasis of tranquility surrounded as it is by the chaos that is now Calcutta. In the good old days tea planters, British colonials of every rank, and their guests filed into the hallowed halls of this social club in search of familiar ideas, friends, and food. Indians were not admitted as members. Now all this has changed and most of the membership is Indian.

The Victoria Memorial, Calcutta

The Bengal Club in 1867, Calcutta

Footnotes to history as I see it: The club is a large, impressive ochre-colored mansion of the eighteenth- and nineteenth-century style of architecture typical of the many grand houses of the colonial period. Now, most of these villas have deteriorated, except for the club, which retains a firm grip on the past.

A teakwood board lists the past presidents of the Bengal Club from the first in 1827, a Lt. Colonel, the Right Honorable J. Finch, C.B., whose name has disappeared into colonial history. The sideboard at the entrance to the office was once the property of Field Marshal Earl Kitchener of Khartoum fame, Commander in Chief in India from 1902–1909.

The large guestroom as one enters the club from the cobra at the main entrance is an impressive space for receptions and meetings. It is filled with antique lithographs and oil paintings of important English personalities of the day.

Along the staircase, which leads up to the dining room and the sixteen commodious rooms available for guests, who must be introduced by a member, are a collection of 15 celebrated lithographs of Calcutta drawn by William Woods about 1830. All around are the artifacts of the colonial period. A stuffed water buffalo head with an enormous horn spread, a cage elevator now properly electrified to be self-operating, and fine wood tables, cabinets, chairs, and carved doors are all in good taste and impressive.

My suite consisted of a large sitting room furnished with typical, oversized bulky chairs and settees of another era. The bedroom with its ubiquitious overhead punkha (ceiling fan) had a large teakwood almirah for clothes, shoes, and the like. A bathroom with the necessary archaic equipment and plumbing was utilitarian. A balcony overlooked the garden and was a lookout for the cackling crows scavenging bits of toast from my early morning breakfast. The personal room servant assigned to me for the visit remembered me during my residence on Camac Street. Nostalgia!

At a recent lunch in the club, the dining room was impeccably furnished, the staff vigilant but not intrusive, the service of a professionalism that stretched back to the colonial days. The food was excellent Anglo-Indian fare: a rich tomato soup, an herb omelette, a remarkable chicken curry and rice, sweet mango chutney, and a blancmange dessert that combined the cooking of England and India. All was calm, cool, tranquil, and of another world.

Outside on the street, Calcutta carried on in its own unique way. But back to the food!

SHRIMP AND BAMBOO SHOOT CURRY
A MONSOON CURRY

In my opinion, this is one of the finest of all Indian curries, a recipe gleaned from the archives of the Bengal Club in Calcutta, India, where I lived for several years. This famous club, situated in the English center of the city, is a large, imposing structure characteristic of the colonial architecture of the eighteenth and nineteenth centuries. The insignia of the club, which is imbedded in the marble entrance floor, was that of a deadly cobra aroused and coiled. The same insignia was painted on the china in the dining room and imprinted on the club stationery.

I was privileged to spend several days in one of the club's sixteen rooms available for guests, who must be introduced by a member in good standing. All around the many rooms of the club were artifacts of the British colonial period, a sideboard in the office was once the property of Field Marshal Earl Kitchener of Khartoum. A cage elevator, now properly electrified and self-operating, took guests to the dining room and other floors.

Nostalgia for the "old India hands," of which I was one, was the order of the day. Turbaned bearers, the table and room servants, glided barefoot, soundlessly, through the corridors on errands for the guests. A large water buffalo head with an enormous horn spread commanded one wall. Along the polished teak staircase the celebrated nineteenth-century lithographs of William Woods and the Oriental scenery aquatints of Thomas and William Daniell (I have several in my private collection) covered the walls. They are the colonial footnotes to Indian history.

Within the club precincts and extensive garden, meticulously groomed by the *mali* (gardener), all was serene and civilized in the English fashion. Outside on the streets, the stupefying heat covered the city. Was it any wonder that Rudyard Kipling wrote his famous description of the city, *Calcutta—Where the cholera, the cyclone, and the Crow / Come and go*. Those who really know Calcutta loved it as I did once, warts and all.

The chief steward of the Club opened an old ledger that held the curry recipes that I duly recorded and dined on during my days as a guest. Shrimp and bamboo curry was my first curry in India and I have never forgotten its startling impact, a revelation, in fact, for its variety of textures, flavors, and aromas that assailed my nostrils—an addiction that I have never been able to cure. Here is the curry.

2 *pounds medium shrimp, peeled and deveined*
2 *tablespoons lemon juice*
1 *teaspoon salt*
4 *tablespoons peanut or corn oil*
1 *medium onion, chopped fine (3/4 cup)*
4 *cloves garlic, chopped fine*
1 *inch fresh ginger, chopped fine*
3/4 *cup chopped fresh tomato, or canned*
1 *teaspoon ground cumin*
1 *teaspoon ground coriander*
1 *teaspoon turmeric*
1 *tablespoon hot red chili flakes, or less to taste*
4 *cups fresh or canned bamboo shoots, sliced into thin julienne strips*
1 *cup fresh coconut milk plus the coconut water if available*
3 *tablespoons chopped fresh coriander for garnish*

1. Marinate the shrimp in the lemon juice and salt for 1 hour.
2. Heat the oil in a pan (a *dekshi* in Calcutta), add the onion, and stir-fry it over moderate heat until it turns light brown. Add the garlic and ginger and stir-fry another minute. Add the tomato and mix well.
3. Add the cumin, coriander, turmeric, and chili flakes and stir for a minute or two to integrate all the seasonings. Add the shrimp and marinade, bamboo shoots, and the coconut milk and water. Simmer the mixture over low heat for 15–20 minutes. Adjust the salt if necessary.

   Remove the pan from the heat, cover, and let stand for 10 minutes, which allows the coconut milk to be absorbed by the shrimp and bamboo shoots. Garnish with the fresh coriander. Serve warm with white rice and a variety of table chutneys and pickles.

Serves 6.

NOTE: In the event that you are unable to prepare fresh coconut milk and reserve the coconut water, then use canned coconut milk imported from Thailand plus 1/2 cup plain water as a substitute.

When the monsoon rains used to start in Calcutta during the middle of June, the groves of bamboo in the surrounding tropical countryside would produce the bamboo shoots that were cut when about 20 inches high. My cook would check the famous nineteenth-century New Market, the huge sprawling market in central Calcutta, for the first arrival of the shoots. Fresh bamboo is first peeled, then cut into thin, matchstick julienne slices about 3 inches long. They are soaked in cold water for an hour to remove the slightly bitter taste, and well drained. Then they are ready to include in the curry. Canned bamboo shoots are better than nothing and can be substituted for the fresh shoots, which are hard to come by in the United States.

Canned bamboo shoots must be rinsed well in cold water before using.

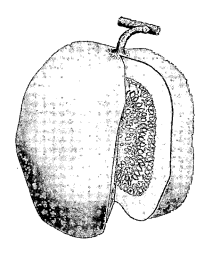

SHRIMP AND
VEGETABLE CURRY

This recipe was given to me by the chief steward of the Bengal Club in Calcutta, where it was taken from the archives. The club itself, filled with all the artifacts of British colonial life, was a mecca for the tea planters who came down out of the hills to experience good Anglo-Indian food, scotch and soda, gin and ginger, among the libations that were reputed to eliminate nostalgia for England and kill the microbes that bedeviled the Europeans and the American culinary reporter who was working in India at that time.

When I lived and worked in Calcutta, my cook used to buy fresh shrimp, alive and jumping, during the rainy monsoon months, which stretched from June to September. This guaranteed freshness during a period when refrigeration was available but not always as efficient as it should have been.

2 *pounds medium shrimp, peeled and deveined*
2 *tablespoons lemon juice*
1 *teaspoon salt*
4 *tablespoons peanut or corn oil*
2 *cups cauliflower florets, cut into 1-inch pieces*
2 *cups peeled white pumpkin, cut into 1-inch cubes (see Notes)*
1 *cup fresh green peas or frozen, thawed*
6 *small new potatoes, about 2 inches in length, peeled and halved*
1 *fresh tomato, chopped (3/4 cup)*
1 *medium onion, chopped fine (3/4 cup)*
4 *cloves garlic, chopped fine*
1 *inch fresh ginger, chopped fine*
1/2 *teaspoon ground cumin*
1 *teaspoon ground coriander*
2–3 *teaspoons hot red chili flakes or powder, to taste*
1 *teaspoon turmeric*
1 *cup coconut milk plus 1/4 cup water*
1 *fresh young coconut (optional, see Notes), remove the soft, melting pulp and process until smooth*

1. Marinate the shrimp with the lemon juice and salt for 1 hour in the refrigerator.
2. Put 2 tablespoons of the oil in a pan, add the cauliflower, pumpkin, green peas, and potatoes and sauté them over moderate heat for 3 minutes. Add the tomato and sauté 2 minutes more. (This will partially cook the vegetables.) Set aside.
3. Put the remaining 2 tablespoons oil in another pan and over moderate heat stir-fry the onion, garlic, and ginger for 2 minutes to lightly brown them. Add the cumin, coriander, chili, and turmeric and mix well for 1 minute. At this point, add 1 tablespoon water to moisten the mixture.
4. Now add the shrimp and marinade to the spice mixture and stir-fry for 3 minutes. Add the salt and vegetables, cover the pan and steam fry for 3 minutes to soften everything. Add the coconut milk, water and the soft pulp from a young coconut, if available. Simmer the entire mixture over low heat, uncovered, for 10 minutes to integrate the flavors and allow the coconut milk to be absorbed by the shrimp and vegetables. Serve warm with white rice or seasoned pilau, chutneys and pickles of your choice.

Serves 6.

NOTES: The white pumpkin, also known to many as winter melon *(Benincasa hispida)*, is a common sight in New York's Chinatown. It is a very large green melon, weighing 5–10 pounds and is frequently covered with white powder. The merchants cut the melon and sell it by the pound. Its white flesh adds a nice crunch to the curry and a modest touch of sweetening.

Wherever I traveled around India during the many years I lived there, I was able to find stands selling young green coconuts. It was not safe to drink the water anywhere and I never did. But the coconut water was cool, refreshing, and safe. Afterward, one could open the coconut and scoop out the soft, melting, white sweet pulp and have a good snack.

PRAWN CURRY
(CIRCA 1915)

> Prawn is the name by which shrimp are known in Calcutta and the waterways of the state of Bengal. This recipe is as simple to make in 1996 as it was in 1915.

3 tablespoons ghee *(clarified butter) or peanut oil*
1 medium onion, sliced (1/2 cup)
1 tablespoon Calcutta Curry Powder (page 159)
1 pound medium prawns, peeled and deveined
1/2 teaspoon salt, or to taste
1 cup hot water
1 teaspoon garam masala *(see Glossary)*

1. Heat the *ghee* or oil in a pan, add the onion, and stir-fry it over moderate heat until light brown. Add the curry powder and stir well. Add the prawns and fry for 2 minutes until "well browned," that is to say, cooked.
2. Add the salt and water and simmer the mixture for 10 minutes over low heat. Sprinkle the *garam masala* over all. Serve warm.

Serves 4 with rice and chapati.

NOTE: To prepare the Bengal Club *garam masala*, take 2 cardamom pods, 4 whole cloves, and 1/2 inch cinnamon stick and very lightly toast them over low heat in a dry skillet for about 3 minutes, until the aroma rises. Then grind to a powder.

FISH CURRY
BENGAL CLUB
STYLE

Fish is king in Calcutta and in the state of Bengal, where it is cheap and plentiful. Water is everywhere as the various estuaries of the Ganges empty into the Bay of Bengal some sixty miles south of the city. The Hooghly River, nicknamed, "the ugly ooghly," carries the silt from the Himalayan highlands, passing Calcutta on its way to the sea. Within the city of Calcutta itself tanks or ponds are scattered everywhere, some of them one or two blocks in size, or more. They are an essential source of water to many of the inhabitants. The one on Albert Road, two blocks from my house, was a placid sheet of water that harbored carp and was a breeding ground for mosquitoes.

The most popular fish is *betki*, a large white-fleshed sea fish similar to sea bass. One could buy thick slices, the fillet, or the whole fish for special occasions. My cook would purchase *betki* automatically, since it was the fish of choice of the Europeans who lived and worked in Calcutta. Here is an Anglo-Indian method of cooking fish from the Bengal Club, the last bastion of English life in Calcutta.

  2 *pound whole sea bass, red snapper, porgy, or similar saltwater fish*
  2 *tablespoons lemon juice*
1/2 *teaspoon salt*
  1 *teaspoon ground cumin*
  1 *teaspoon ground coriander*
  1 *inch fresh ginger, sliced*
  2 *cloves garlic, sliced*
  1 *medium onion, sliced (3/4 cup)*
  4 *tablespoons peanut or corn oil*
  1 *cup chopped fresh tomato, or canned*
1/2 *teaspoon turmeric*
2 or 3 *teaspoons hot red chili flakes, to taste*
  1 *cup coconut milk*
1/2 *teaspoon* garam masala (*see* Glossary) *for garnish*

1. Clean the fish in the conventional manner, but do not remove the head or tail. Score the fish on the diagonal twice on each side. Mix the lemon juice, salt, cumin, and coriander together and rub this into the incisions. Set aside for 1 hour.
2. Prepare the sauce: Process the ginger, garlic, and onion to a smooth paste, adding 2 tablespoons water to moisten the mixture as you do. You may also grind the mixture in a mortar and pestle. (My cook in Calcutta reduced spices and seasonings to a smooth paste on an antique stone tablet with a round, stone hand-grinder. This is the traditional method not only for Indians, but with the Mayans of Guatemala where I worked for some years.)
3. Heat 2 tablespoons oil in a pan or large skillet, add the spice paste, and stir-fry it over moderate heat about 1 minute, to change the color without burning. Add the tomato, turmeric, and chili flakes and continue to stir-fry for another minute. Then add the coconut milk, bring to a boil, and simmer the sauce over low heat for 10 minutes as you prepare the fish.
4. Heat the remaining 2 tablespoons oil in another skillet and fry the fish on both sides over moderate heat just enough to lightly brown but not completely cook it. About 2 or 3 minutes should be sufficient. At this stage you have two possible ways to complete the cooking:

    The first is to add the half-fried fish to the sauce in the pan or skillet and continue to simmer over low heat, covered, for 20 minute, basting now and then. Sprinkle with the *garam masala* over before serving.

    The second method is to put the sauce into an oiled Pyrex or metal baking dish. Add the fish and bake in a preheated 350 degree oven for 20 minutes, basting several times. Sprinkle with the *garam masala*. Serve with white rice and an assortment of table chutneys and pickles.

Serves 6.

COUNTRY CAPTAIN CURRY

At the Bengal Club several recipes from their archives, which, alas, no longer exist, were gleaned from the heading, Indian Dishes for Bengal Club Tables, from about 1915.

Country captain curry was well known in those days, as were the country captains whose ships plied the lanes from India to China. As told to me by a Bengali merchant marine of a certain age, the curry was sometimes a breakfast dish and, as it was easy to prepare on sea or on land, became well known.

1 small chicken (2 pounds)
4 tablespoons ghee (clarified butter) or peanut oil
1/2 pound onion, sliced thin (1 cup)
1/2 teaspoon hot red chili powder
1/2 teaspoon turmeric
1 teaspoon salt, or to taste
1 cup water
1/2 teaspoon black cuminseed (kalajira, available in Indian markets), toasted in a dry skillet and ground to a powder

1. Cut the chicken into 8 pieces, according to your preference. Heat the *ghee* or oil in a pan and stir-fry the onion over low heat until brown and crisp. Do not burn. Remove and set aside.
2. Add the chili powder and turmeric and stir-fry rapidly for 1/2 minute. Add the chicken pieces and salt and continue to stir until the pink color has disappeared. Add the water, bring to a boil, add the browned onions, and simmer until the liquid has been absorbed. (The chicken will be tender and have a thick sauce.) Sprinkle with the toasted cuminseed. Serve warm with rice and sweet mango chutney.

Serves 4.

Pish Pash
(or The Doctor's Advice)

This gruel is recommended when experiencing a "tummy" upset so prevalent in India or other illnesses when appetite fails.

1 1/2 pounds boneless lamb, cut into 1/4-inch cubes, well rinsed
3–4 cups cold water
  1 cup rice, well rinsed and drained
  1 teaspoon salt, or to taste
  2 whole cloves
  4 peppercorns
  1 inch cinnamon stick

Put the lamb and water in a pan, bring to a boil, and cook over moderate heat for 1/2 hour to almost soften the meat. Add the rice, salt, cloves, peppercorns, and cinnamon stick and cook for another 20 minutes, to the consistency of a gruel without much liquid. (Should the water be absorbed or evaporate too quickly, add another 1/2 cup hot water to soften the meat and rice.) Serve warm.

Serves 4.

JHALFARAZIE OF COOKED MEATS, CHICKEN, OR FISH
Dry and Spicy Curry

This is more-or-less a method of utilizing leftovers. Some cooks prefer to use at least two kinds of meat and fish.

2 tablespoons ghee (clarified butter) or vegetable oil
1 small onion, sliced thin (1/3 cup)
1 tablespoon curry powder
1/2 teaspoon hot red chili powder or thinly sliced hot green chili
1/4 cup cooked beef, lamb, chicken, or fish, cut into 1/2-inch cubes
1/2 teaspoon salt
1/4 cup water

Heat the *ghee* or oil in a pan and stir-fry the onion over moderate heat until crisp and light brown. Do not burn. Add the curry powder, chili, and the cooked meat or fish and mix well. Add the salt and water and cook for 5 minutes as a rich, brown sauce develops. Serve warm with rice.

Serves 2.

COCONUT RICE PUDDING

Another recipe from the old days, when English ladies preferred something familiar.

1/4 cup dessicated coconut
1 cup boiling water
1/2 cup rice, soaked in cold water 1 hour and drained
1/2 cup milk
1/2 cup sugar
1 very small bay leaf
2 cardamom pods
2 tablespoons raisins

1. Put the coconut in a bowl, pour the boiling water over it, cover, and let stand for 1 hour. Strain the mixture through a metal strainer into a bowl and press out all the liquid. Discard the coconut and reserve the liquid.
2. Put the rice and coconut liquid into a pan and simmer over low heat for 10 minutes. Add the milk, sugar, bay leaf, cardamom pods, and raisins and cook over low heat for 10 minutes, or until the mixture is thick. Serve warm.

Serves 4.

CALCUTTA CURRY POWDER

1 teaspoon turmeric
1 tablespoon coriander seed
1 tablespoon poppy seed
1/2 teaspoon ground ginger
1/2 teaspoon hot red chili powder
1/2 teaspoon cuminseed

Grind all the ingredients together in a mini food processor. Store in a glass jar with a tight cover.

Makes about 1/4 cup.

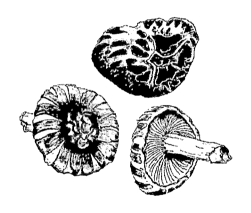

Madras Curry Powder

1/2 teaspoon turmeric
1 teaspoon hot red chili flakes
2 mustard seeds
1/2 teaspoon coriander seed
1/4 teaspoon cuminseed
1/2 teaspoon poppy seed

Grind all the ingredients together in a mini food processor or in a mortar and pestle. Store in a glass jar with a tight cover.

Makes a scant 1/4 cup.

NOTE: These two curry powder recipes were selected from *Dainty Dishes for Indian Tables*, published by W. Newman and Co., 3, Dalhousie Square, Calcutta, 1881.

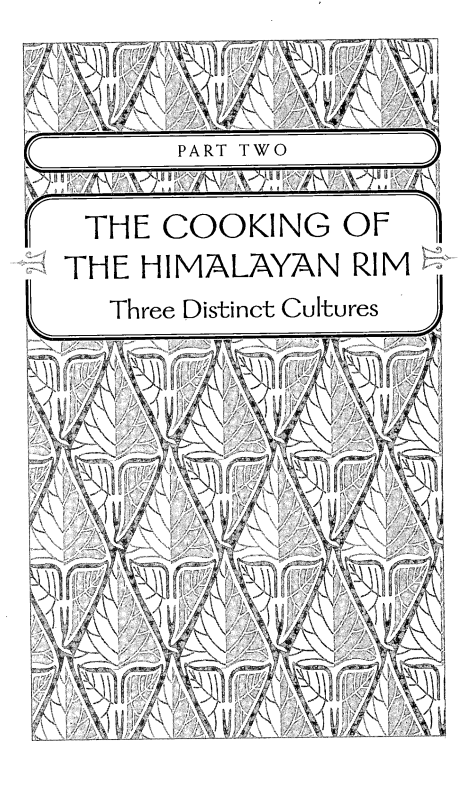

PART TWO

THE COOKING OF
THE HIMALAYAN RIM
Three Distinct Cultures

⚖ 6 ⚖

THE COOKING OF THE
KINGDOM OF BHUTAN

ONCE UPON a time, as the story goes, I was taking a brisk early morning walk (5:30 A.M. when the air was still fresh) on Chowringhee Road, Calcutta's principal street that runs along the Maidan, the large central park. I saw a rickshaw *wallah* pulling with great effort two burly men sitting in a place where only one should have been. They were holding on their laps a metal box that looked as though it contained the national treasury and wearing ornately woven costumes known as the *baku* of dark blue, green, red, and orange. The voluminous sleeves were striking and appeared to be filled with something. (I subsequently added one of these textiles to my collection.)

My neighbor told me they were from Bhutan. They were the first Bhutanese I had ever seen.

Bhutan is situated in the heart of the Himalayas. The northern frontier with Tibet is covered with snow-covered peaks, and the southern border of this tiny landlocked country descends to the tropical lowlands of India. In between are gradations of climate that produce agriculture suitable to the lavish vegetation that covers the area.

Ruled by a king, the Dragon (Druk) Kingdom until recent times was a medieval kingdom that jealously guarded its culture and history from the contamination of foreign influences. With a country without roads and guarded by impassable mountains, alone and secretive, the Bhutanese rulers, guided by the benevolent influence of Buddhism, have produced a liberal democracy. It is open, in its limited way, to tourism, the advantages of the twentieth century, and a new way of life. The Dragon King, the yak, and the Himalayas are eternal.

The countryside is dotted with *dzongs*, which are not only fortresses but also centers of Buddhist activities, and the presence of lamas. Weaving and other handicrafts attest to a sturdy race of people with ancient links to Tibet and similarities in their ways of life. Blessed with the physical beauties of the country, the independent-

Bhutanese dancer (Photo by Desmond Doig)

minded Bhutanese value what could have been the first and perhaps is now the last Shangri-La.

But what of the food? Within the limited range of the cooking of Bhutan, simplicity is the hallmark. When speaking to the Bhutanese, they always remark that their food is, indeed, simple, of the people. One eats to live off the land.

What are the characteristics of Bhutanese food and how does one turn it into a presentable dish? In a few words, onion, ginger, garlic, the fresh or dry hot chili, and Bhutan's ubiquitous fermented cheese. Many foods that are represented with recipes are too chili-hot to be tolerated by many western palates. My suggestion would be to reduce the amount of chili to personal preference and with considerable judicious attention to the quantity.

Pork is the most popular meat, with beef, sometimes yak, and chicken following behind since they are too expensive for the average family. One way of circumventing cost is to utilize the dried strips of beef and pork that are combined with seasonings, greens, noodles, and sometimes tomato and stringbeans. The meat

The flag of Bhutan

is stretched to feed a number of family members with large quantities of rice.

There are actually two classes of cooking. One is for the common man in a medieval society where simple ingredients are combined with the hot chili and the fermented firm white cheese that is available even during the frigid mountain winters. The other style of cooking may be called the royal food or that of the wealthy classes, where cost is no problem and more pork, beef, and chicken is added to the diet. I was fortunate to meet the cook of one of the royal families and learn a number of dishes that were not overloaded with an excessive number of chilis. Modified and tasty combinations were presented to me and are included in this collection.

The most important feature of the cooking of Bhutan, in my opinion, is that a sturdy race has developed within their mountain vastness on simple and flavorful foods that are grown in pristine air and water, geared to the requirements and demands of a Himalayan culture. Is this not an advantage that other countries, large or small, would envy in the polluted and overchemicalized atmosphere of our planet?

T H U K P A
Breakfast Rice Porridge

The highlands of Bhutan are cold in the winter and this richly endowed porridge, peasant food, is not only filling but flavorful as well.

1 *pound pork bones with meat still attached*
5 *cups water*
1 *teaspoon salt, or to taste*
1 *cup rice, well rinsed*
1 *medium onion, chopped (1/2 cup)*
1 *inch fresh ginger, chopped*
1/2–1 *teaspoon red chili powder, to taste*
1 *tablespoon vegetable oil*

Cook the bones in the water with the salt over moderate heat for 1/2 hour. Add the rice and all the remaining ingredients and simmer, uncovered, over low heat for 1 hour. (The rice should become very soft and melting.) If you prefer a less thick porridge, add another cup water. Adjust the salt. Serve the porridge hot with the bones during cold weather.

Serves 6.

M O M O
Stuffed Steamed Dumplings Bhutan Style

Mo mo is probably an invention of the Tibetans with whom the Bhutanese are racially and culturally related. I have eaten many Tibetan *mo mo* in Darjeeling, India, where there is and has been a large encampment for many years. I do not take sides in this culinary conundrum.

THE STUFFING

> *1 pound boneless ground chicken, or beef, or pork*
> *1 large onion, chopped fine (1 cup)*
> *2 inches fresh ginger, peeled and grated*
> *1 sprig fresh coriander (Chinese parsley) leaves and young stems, chopped fine*
> *2 teaspoons salt*
> *1 teaspoon red chili powder*
> *1/2 teaspoon pepper*

THE DOUGH

> *3 1/2–4 cups flour*
> *1/4 teaspoon baking powder*
> *About 1/2 cup cold water*

1. Make the stuffing: Mix all the ingredients together well. Set aside.
2. Make the dough: Mix the flour, baking powder, and enough of the water to produce a firm but malleable dough. Cover and set aside for 30 minutes.
3. Make the dumplings: Pull off 1 heaping tablespoon of the dough and roll it into a ball. Roll the ball out into a 3-inch pancake in which the center is thicker than the outside edges. (The thicker center will support the moist meat within.)
4. Put a nugget, about 1 tablespoon of the stuffing, in the center of the pancake and push up the sides toward the center. Then pinch and turn the edges of the dough in a circle to enclose the stuffing. Finally, twist the top edges of the dumpling 3 or 4 times to close. Roll out pancakes and make dumpling with the remaining ingredients in the same manner.
5. Using a Chinese-style steamer, rub a 1/2 teaspoon of oil over

the perforated surface of the steamer tray. Place the dumplings in the steamer with about 1/2 inch in between. Steam chicken dumplings over moderate heat for 15 minutes; beef dumplings for 20 minutes; and pork dumplings for 25 minutes. Serve warm as an appetizer with a soy sauce dip or a chili hot paste.

Makes 30 dumplings.

K O O L E
Buckwheat Pancakes

Buckwheat flour is used in these simple pancakes, which are served with spiced vegetables. In fact, the Bhutanese of the central region of the country prepare noodles with buckwheat flour and water. The dough is forced through a hand grinder with round holes and the noodles come out round. In Korea fritters, noodles, and pancakes are also made with buckwheat flour. In short, this special flour is not exclusive to Bhutanese cooking.

3 1/2–4 *cups buckwheat flour*
    1 *egg, beaten*
     About 1 cup water
     Vegetable oil for rubbing the skillet

1. Mix the flour, egg, and enough water together to form a pancake batter with conventional consistency.
2. Rub a Teflon skillet with about 1/2 teaspoon vegetable oil and heat the skillet slightly. Pour in 1/4 cup batter and fry the pancake over low heat for 2 minutes on each side. The pancake will be about 3 inches in diameter but can be made smaller or larger according to personal preference. Some cooks prepare a large pancake 12 inches in diameter and cut it like a pie at serving time. Make pancakes with the remaining batter in the same manner. Serve warm with seasoned cooked vegetables.

Makes 12–15 small pancakes.

CHIM CHAMPA
Liver Snack

Pork is the most popular meat in Bhutan and pork liver is utilized more than the beef liver is. However, both are valid in this recipe.

1 pound pork or beef liver, rinsed well in cold water and cut into 2-inch-thin slices
1 teaspoon salt
1 teaspoon red chili powder
1/4 teaspoon black pepper
1 clove garlic, crushed
2 tablespoons vegetable oil
1/4 cup chopped onion
2 cloves garlic, chopped
1 inch fresh ginger, chopped
1 large onion, sliced (1 cup)
1/2 teaspoon Szechuan peppercorn, crushed
1 tablespoon fresh coriander (Chinese parsley) leaves, chopped

1. Mix the pork (or beef) liver together with the salt, chili powder, pepper, and crushed garlic. Set aside.
2. Heat the oil in a wok, add the chopped onion, and stir-fry over moderate heat for 1 minute. Add the chopped garlic and ginger and stir-fry for 2 minutes.
3. Add the liver mixture and stir-fry until the color changes, about 3 minutes. Add the sliced onion and continue to stir-fry until the onion has softened, another 2 minutes. Scatter the peppercorn and coriander over the entire mixture. Serve warm as a snack with drinks or as an additional dish with a meal.

Serves 6.

KYOWA DASI
Potato Curry with Cheese

This spicy curry, chili-hot, is treated as a soup and one of the dishes in a meal. Especially welcome in winter.

3 or 4 potatoes (1 pound), peeled and sliced into rounds
6 small hot green chilis, cut halfway open lengthwise
1 tablespoon vegetable oil
1/2 teaspoon salt, or to taste
1 1/2 cups water
1/4 pound Bhutanese-style cheese, sliced or grated
3 cloves garlic, sliced thin

1. Put the potatoes, chilis, oil, salt, and water in a pan and bring to a boil. Cook over moderate heat to soften the ingredients for 10 minutes.
2. Add the cheese and garlic and cook for 3 minutes. Cover the pan and let stand off the heat for 10 minutes until ready to serve. Stir well. The soup will be creamy in appearance because the cheese melts. Serve in small bowls with rice.

Serves 6.

EMA DASI
Rotten Cheese

A Bhutanese princess jokingly referred to the common type of cheese used in daily cooking as rotten, since it contains a degree of fermentation. In fact, it is similar to a firmly pressed farmer's cheese and is preserved for use during the long winter months. A Tibetan friend used a mixture of Roquefort-type cheese mixed with farmer's cheese to obtain its fermented characteristic.

1/4 pound Bhutanese-style cheese
1 1/2 cups water
1/4 pound hot green chilis, halved lengthwise
1/2 teaspoon salt
1 large fresh tomato, coarsely chopped (1 cup)
1 tablespoon vegetable oil
3 cloves garlic, chopped

1. Coarsely chop the cheese. Bring 1 cup of the water to a boil in a pan, add the chilis, and cook for 5 minutes. Drain. (This blanching reduces the chili heat and was done for my benefit when I gasped at the amount of chilis in this recipe. The Bhutanese will not gasp as they prefer all the spice they can get.)
2. Put the chilis, cheese, the remaining 1/2 cup water, salt, tomato, oil, and garlic in a pan, cover, and cook over low heat for 5 minutes. Some liquid will evaporate and the sauce will thicken. Serve warm with rice.

Serves 6.

N O S H A P H I N
Beef with Rice Noodles

1 1/2 *pounds tender beef steak (tenderloin), cut into thin slices, 1 inch long and 1/4 inch wide*
   1 *medium onion, chopped (1/2 cup)*
   3 *cloves garlic, crushed*
   2 *inches fresh ginger, peeled and chopped fine*
   1 *teaspoon red chili powder*
   1 *teaspoon salt, or to taste*
   2 *tablespoons vegetable oil*
1 1/2 *cups water*
   3 *ounces thick dried rice noodles, covered with boiling water 5 minutes, drained, and cut into 2-inch pieces*
1 or 2 *hot green chilis, seeded and sliced (optional)*
   2 *scallions, green part only, cut into 1-inch pieces*

1. Put the beef, onion, garlic, ginger, chili powder, salt, and oil in a pan with 1/2 cup of the water. Cook over moderate heat for 10 minutes until the liquid evaporates. Stir-fry for 2 minutes in the oil as the color of the beef changes.
2. Add the remaining 1 cup water and cook for 1/2 hour, until the meat is tender and there is substantial sauce. Add the *phin* (noodles) and green chilis if you wish to increase the "heat" of the curry. When ready to serve, stir in the scallions. Serve warm.

Serves 8.

NO GEE CHAE
DA LEP
Brain and Beef Tongue Combination

I am particularly fond of brain and tongue and deliberately search out recipes in the culture I'm researching. The Bhutanese, too, enjoy these innards. As occurs frequently, each is cooked separately, then are mixed together and served as a melange. If combined, the dish serves eight.

THE BRAIN

1–1 1/2 *pounds beef brain*
   2 *tablespoons butter*
   1 *medium onion, chopped fine (1/2 cup)*
   2 *cloves garlic, chopped fine*
   1 *inch fresh ginger, peeled and chopped fine*
   1 *teaspoon red chili powder*
   1 *teaspoon salt, or to taste*
 1/4 *cup hot water*
   4 *Szechuan peppercorns*
   6 *fresh coriander (Chinese parsley) leaves*

1. Rinse the brain in cold water. Pull off the thin membrane that covers it. Divide the brain in 3 sections and slice each section into 1-inch thin slices.
2. Melt the butter in a pan, add the onion, and stir-fry it 1 minute. Add the garlic, ginger, chili powder, salt, and brain slices. Stir-fry over low heat for 3 minutes. Add the hot water and cook for 15 minutes. Stir in the peppercorns. Before serving, add the coriander. Serve warm.

Serves 4.

THE TONGUE

> *1 veal or beef tongue (2 pounds)*
> *1 cup hot water*

1. Cook the tongue and water in a pressure cooker over low heat for 45 minutes. Remove the tongue, peel it, and discard the skin. The tongue will be tender. Cut the tongue into 1-inch thin slices, the same size, more or less, as the slices of brain.
2. Prepare the tongue in the same manner with the same ingredients called for in Step 2 of the brain recipe. Serve warm.

Serves 4 or more.

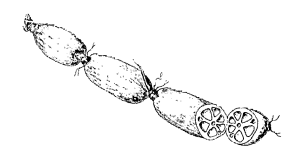

N O   S H A   P A
Dried Beef Curry

Hard, dried unsalted beef strips are one of the principal ingredients in the cooking of Bhutan. The long, slender, boneless strips of beef, and less frequently, yak, about one inch in width, are hung on a line and left out to dry in the sun for about five days.

Much-prized pork is also used, but it is dried in the winter in the cold rarified air and takes longer, about two weeks to air-dry. Pork is not dried in the summer as the fat on it would melt.

Dried beef is used in this curry. This recipe is included for historical purposes, and the hope is that you will be able to find dried beef in the markets that carry it.

1/2 pound dried beef, cut into 2-inch lengths
1 1/2 cups water
3 tablespoons vegetable oil
1/2 pound string beans, cut halfway open
10 fresh or dried hot green or red chilis, cut halfway open lengthwise
1/2 teaspoon salt ·
3 cloves garlic, sliced

1. Cook the beef over low heat in the water for 1/2 hour to soften it. Add the oil, beans, chilis, and salt, cover the pan, and simmer for 10 minutes.
2. Add the garlic, stir well, and cook over low heat for 1/2 hour, or until nearly all the liquid has evaporated. Serve warm with rice.

Serves 6.

NOTE: *Saag* (green leaves such as spinach), gathered in the wild, are also used in this dish, in which case use 4–6 ounces and omit the beans.

PHIN STIM
Dried Beef Curry with Rice Noodles

The firm, wiry dried rice noodles used in this recipe require soaking in warm water so that they can be cut (with a scissors) into manageable lengths. Dried beef and green chilis are the other important ingredients in this simple dish.

The hot green chilis used here are the long (3 to 4 inches) "elephant trunk" chilis, so called because they resemble the trunk of an elephant and are a little twisted, being thick at one end and thin at the other. It can be considered a semi-hot chili.

1/2 pound dried beef, cut into 1/4-inch pieces
1 1/2 cups water
1 teaspoon salt
1 tablespoon vegetable oil
10 hot green chilis, such as elephant trunk chilis (see Glossary), halved lengthwise and quartered
3 ounces medium thickness dried rice noodles, soaked in warm water for 5 minutes and drained
1 small fresh tomato, sliced (1/3 cup)

1. Cook the beef with the water, salt, and oil in a pan over moderate heat for 20 minutes, or until the beef is soft. Add the chilis and cook for 2 minutes.
2. Cut the softened noodles into 3-inch lengths and add to the pan with the tomato; simmer for another minute. (The noodles will absorb much of the liquid.) Serve warm in small portions.

Serves 8.

NO SHA TSIDO PA
Ribs of Beef Curry

Here is a hearty curry Bhutanese style that uses butter (which I recommend reducing the amount of substantially), which the Bhutanese like to pour on. Ginger, garlic, and hot chili powder are what give these ribs their character.

2 *pounds beef rib tips, cut into 3-inch pieces, including bone*
2 *cups hot water*
1 *large onion, chopped (1 cup)*
2 *inches fresh ginger, peeled and smashed*
4 *cloves garlic, crushed*
1/2 *pound butter (not oil)*
1 *teaspoon red chili powder*
1 *teaspoon salt, or to taste*
2 *scallions, white part only*

1. Put the beef ribs in 1 cup of the hot water in a pan and cook over moderate heat for 1/2 hour.
2. Add the onion, ginger, garlic, butter, chili powder, and salt and stir-fry for 5 minutes to brown the meat. Add the remaining 1 cup hot water and cook over low heat, covered, until the beef is tender, about 1 hour more. (Nearly all the liquid will evaporate and the small amount of buttered sauce will be brown.) Stir in the scallions. Serve warm.

Serves 8.

TSASHA MARO
Chicken Curry

Meat costs money and chicken is the food of the upper classes or the wealthy in Bhutan. The word curry is used by most communities in Asia and Southeast Asia, having taken the lead from India.

1 1/2 *pounds Cornish hen or chicken parts*
1 1/4 *cups hot water*
   1 *medium onion, chopped (1/2 cup)*
   3 *cloves garlic, chopped*
   1 *inch fresh ginger, peeled, smashed, and chopped*
   1 *teaspoon salt, or to taste*
   1 *teaspoon red chili powder*
   1 *tablespoon butter*
 1/4 *cup chopped peeled fresh tomato*
 10 *fresh coriander (Chinese parsley) leaves for garnish*

1. Cut the Cornish hen through the bone into 2-inch pieces. (Or, use the equivalent in boneless chicken, cut into 1-inch cubes.)
2. Put the meat in a pan with 1/4 cup of the water and cook over low heat for 10 minutes. Add the onion, garlic, ginger, salt, chili powder, and butter and stir-fry the chicken for 3 minutes, until brown.
3. Add the remaining 1 cup hot water and tomato and simmer for 1/2 hour. Taste and increase the chili powder if desired (the Bhutanese would) and the salt. Garnish with the coriander. Serve warm.

Serves 6.

TSASHA STOOSTO
Chicken Roast

Chicken is one of the meats of the wealthy in Bhutan and this is a simple method of preparing it. The roasting is done on top of the stove because so few kitchens have baking (roasting) ovens.

1 cup water
2 pounds chicken parts—thighs, legs, breasts, cut into 4 pieces—or a Cornish hen, quartered
2 inches fresh ginger, halved lengthwise
1 teaspoon salt
1 tablespoon butter

1. Put everything, except the butter, in a pan, cover, and cook over low heat until nearly all the liquid has evaporated, turning the pieces over now and then, about 1/2 hour.
2. Then brown the chicken pieces for 5 minutes in the butter and chicken fat in the pan. Serve warm.

Serves 4 with other Bhutanese dishes.

NYA TSEM
Hot Fish Curry

Bhutan has a number of rivers that are well filled with water from the melting snow of the Himalayas. Trout and other freshwater varieties abound and this curry is one way of preparing them. For this purpose, fresh or saltwater fish may be used, with a judicious amount of green chilis.

12 small fresh hot green chilis, halved lengthwise
1 inch fresh ginger, sliced, then smashed
3 cloves garlic, crushed
1 cup water
1 small fresh tomato, sliced (1/2 cup)
2 tablespoons mustard oil or vegetable oil
1 teaspoon salt, or to taste
    A 3-pound fresh or saltwater whole fish, sliced 1 inch thick
1/2 cup farmer's cheese, crumbled

1. Put the chilis, ginger, garlic, water, tomato, oil, and salt in a large pan and bring to a boil. Simmer for 10 minutes over moderate heat.
2. Add the fish and cook, covered, for 10 minutes. Add the cheese, shake the pan briskly to combine the ingredients, and cook for 10 minutes more. Serve warm.

Serves 8 with rice.

P ᴀ K S H ᴀ P ᴀ
Hot Pork Curry

> Pork is the most popular meat in Bhutan, and this pork curry is the most popular way of preparing it. Like most Bhutanese dishes, the fresh hot green chilis in more than modest numbers are mandatory. The pork here cooks with ginger but not garlic.

 3 *pounds pork ribs with bone, cut into 3-inch pieces*
 1 *teaspoon salt*
 1 *cup water*
 1 *pound Chinese white radish (daikon)*
15 *fresh elephant trunk chilis (see Glossary), or less to taste, halved lengthwise*
 1 *inch fresh ginger, peeled, sliced, then smashed*

1. Cook the pork with the salt in the water in a pressure cooker until soft, about 20 minutes. (My Bhutanese cooking teacher, in fact, preferred this method.) Or, cook it for 1 hour on the top of the stove. In that case, double the amount of water.
2. Add the radish to the pressure cooker and cook without pressure for 5 minutes. Add the chilis and cook over moderate heat until nearly all the liquid has evaporated, about 20 minutes. Stir in the ginger and remove the pan from the heat. Let stand 10 minutes, covered, before serving. Serve warm with rice.

Serves 8.

PA SHA LAMENDA
Pork and Tomato Curry

Pork and tomato make a good combination in this Bhutanese curry. There is no garlic here; fresh ginger provides the pork with its principal seasoning. Like all Bhutanese cooking, there are not a lot of complicated steps or ingredients. Simplicity is part of the cuisine.

3 *cups water*
1 *pound boneless pork, cut into 1-inch cubes*
1 *inch fresh ginger, peeled and firmly smashed*
1 *small onion, chopped (1/3 cup)*
1 *teaspoon salt*
1/4– 1/2 *teaspoon red chili powder*
4 *small tomatoes (3/4 pound), peeled and quartered*

1. Bring the water to a boil in a pan and add the pork, ginger, onion, salt, and chili powder. Cook over moderate heat for 1/2 hour.
2. Add the tomatoes, stir to combine, and simmer for 10 minutes more, or until the pork is tender. This is a curry to be eaten with rice and has sufficient sauce. Serve warm.

Serves 6.

A Y Z A Y
Dynamic Table Condiment

2 tablespoons red chili powder or dried chili flakes
1 medium onion, chopped (1/2 cup)
1 teaspoon salt
1/4 cup water, or enough to produce a thick paste

Grind everything together in a food processor into a not-too-smooth paste. Serve at teatime with dried meat, beef or pork, butter, and the dried rice known as *zow*.

Makes about 1/4 cup.

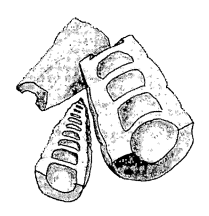

HENSTAY
Hot Chili, Leaf Greens, and Cheese

This simple but traditional Bhutanese preparation contains the quintessential hot chili, *saag* (garden greens), and cheese, common everyday foods of these mountain people.

1 cup water
1 tablespoon vegetable oil
1 teaspoon salt
4 whole green chilis
1/2 pound spinach leaves, mustard greens, or another green-leaf vegetable
2 tablespoons crumbled farmer's cheese

1. Cook the water, oil, salt, and chilis together in a pan for 5 minutes. (Be aware that the chilis will release a powerfully pungent aroma that results in considerable sneezing and tearing on the part of the cook.)
2. Add the greens and simmer over moderate heat for 3 minutes. Add the cheese and stir to melt, about 2 minutes. Serve warm as a side dish.

Serves 4.

DAYSEE
Sweet Festival Rice

This is plain white rice that is combined with raisins, saffron (for color), sugar, and melted butter as an attractive sweet that is served with Butter Tea (page 192) during festivals of any kind in Bhutan.

2 *cups plain white cooked rice, warm*
1 *tablespoon sugar or more to taste*
3 *tablespoons raisins*
3 *tablespoons melted butter*
3–4 *dried saffron stigmas*

Dissolve saffron in one teaspoon of warm water. Combine rest of ingredients and serve with Butter Tea (page 192).

Serves 4.

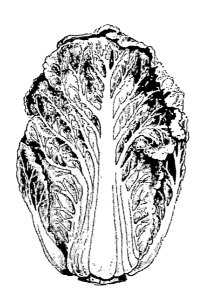

MITAKOPI DASI
Cauliflower and Cheese

A tasty side dish in the Bhutanese style.

1 pound cauliflower, cut into 1-inch florets
1/2 cup water
1 small hot green chili, seeded and quartered
1/2 teaspoon salt
2 tablespoons butter
3 tablespoons farmer's cheese, crumbled

Cook the cauliflower in the water over moderate heat for 2 minutes, shaking the pan vigorously. Add the chili and salt and cook for 2 minutes more. Add the butter and cheese and cook for 1 minute. Mix well to combine and serve warm.

Serves 6.

H O G Y
Cucumber Salad

No dressing here, only a few ingredients, with enough chili to galvanize the tastebuds.

1 *large cucumber, peeled*
1 *small hot green chili, sliced thin*
1 *medium onion, sliced thin*
1/2 *teaspoon salt*
2 *tablespoons crumbled farmer's cheese*

1. Cut the cucumber in half lengthwise and scoop out and discard the seeds. Slice into very thin half-moons.
2. Combine all the ingredients. Serve with any kind of Bhutanese food.

Serves 4.

KENCHU HOGY
Mixed Cucumber Salad with Farmer's Cheese

1 pound small cucumbers
1 small hot green chili, seeded and finely chopped (2 teaspoons)
1 tablespoon fresh coriander (Chinese parsley) leaves
3 tablespoons farmer's cheese, crumbled
2 tablespoons sliced tomato (optional)
1 teaspoon salt

1. Peel the cucumbers and cut into 2-inch-long slivers.
2. Toss all the ingredients at serving time so as not to discolor the salad. The salt should be added last as it draws liquid from the cucumbers, which is not desirable. Serve at room temperature.

Serves 6.

LABOO CHAMPA
Liver and White Radish Salad

Mild white radish provides texture and the liver a meaty substance in this unconventional salad. The Szechuan peppercorn, a rare spice in the Asian firmament, provides a taste surprise.

1/4 pound pork or beef liver
1 pound Chinese white radish (daikon), peeled and cut into thin, short slivers 1 inch long and 1/4 inch wide
1 teaspoon red chili powder, or more or less, to taste
1 teaspoon salt
1/2 teaspoon Szechuan peppercorn, toasted in a dry skillet and crushed
1 scallion, green part only, sliced thin
1 tablespoon ajowan (see Glossary), toasted in a dry skillet and crushed

1. Cook the liver in boiling water over moderate heat 1/2 hour for pork liver and 20 minutes for beef liver. Drain, cool, and cut into thin slivers 1 inch long and 1/4 inch wide.
2. Mix all the ingredients together, except the *ajowan*, and toss well. At serving time, garnish the salad with the *ajowan*. Serve at room temperature.

Serves 6.

S O O J A
Bhutanese Butter Tea

Not to everyone's taste, this traditional tea animates the Bhutanese during the frigid Himalayan winters. *Jari* is the name of the tea that is firmly pressed into triangular cones and sold in this form. Chunks of the cone are broken off and boiled in water so that every bit of essence is utilized during the numerous cups of tea that are drunk over the course of a day.

   3 *cups water*
      A 1-inch chunk pressed tea leaves
   1/8 *teaspoon baking soda*
   1/4 *cup butter, sliced*
      1 *teaspoon salt, or to taste*

Boil the water, tea, and baking soda together over moderate heat for 15 minutes. Strain the mixture into a bowl and discard the tea leaves. Add the butter and whip the mixture for 1 minute until foamy. This can be done in a processor. Add the salt. Drink hot anytime you wish. Serve with various types of sweetened, buttered rice.

Serves 6.

NOTE: Not too many years ago and even today, *sooja* was prepared in a section of bamboo 3 or 4 inches in diameter. Water, tea and butter were shaken or pounded together, strained, and drunk—by the gallon!

⊰ 7 ⊱

THE FLAVORS OF SIKKIM

The era is over! The king is dead! And the storybook fable of the American girl who married the king and went to live in the palace in Gangtok, the capital city of Sikkim, has receded into the distant past. The kingdom of Sikkim was annexed by India in 1975 and has become another one of its states.

That is not the end of the story, since I went to Gangtok to search for the king's cook and found him. His name was Phuchung Lepcha, a small, quick man who knew everything there was to know about the cuisine of Sikkim. The story, or my story, now begins again.

Sikkim is that small country/state sandwiched in between the Himalayan highlands of Nepal on the western flank, Tibet to the north, Bhutan to the east, and India to the south. The Tibetans call it "the land of the rice." With tropical forests and mists that sometimes cover its green valleys, and overshadowed by Khangchendzonga (Kanchenjunga), one of the world's highest mountains, Sikkim is the Buddhist land of the Lepchas, the original inhabitants of the country. There is a legend that circulates that high in the snow-covered mountain peaks is the abode of the Yeti, the Abominable Snowman.

I went there to do research on the cooking habits and food of the people within their Himalayan vastness. From the dry, hot, dusty Indian plain at sea level, the public bus drove up for five hours, twisting and turning on the paved road that ran along the route of the Tista River, which roared downhill to water the soil of India. Finally, we reached Gangtok at 5,800 feet altitude.

Gangtok is built on a steep hill and looks as though a few good earthquake tremors would slide everything and everyone down

The Buddhist Temple, Sikkim

into the valley. This has not happened yet, and this small city remains a microcosm for all types of Himalayan inhabitants from the
surrounding territories. Lepchas, Nepalis, Indians, Tibetans, Bhutanese, and Chinese roam the streets, lending a universal air to the
city.

At the bottom of the hill, one walks down, winding first to
the right, then to the left, descending so that it is almost possible
to touch the head of someone passing on a lower grade. The
marketplace is, in fact, an illustration of the cooking possibili-
ties, but there's no plan at work to separate the edible components
from household necessities. A modest heap of fresh ginger and
onions lie helter skelter next to a small array of razor blades,
matches, shoelaces, and candy bars. Still, one can find what one
came for.

Pork is the most popular meat in Sikkim and it is eaten fresh or
dried. Recipes abound, the price is right, and small amounts of fat

pork ribs can feed even a large family. Beef, chicken, lamb, and fish from the Tista River are found in the market.

Vegetables are luxuriously green and colorful, with *saag* (a local spinach-like plant), nettle leaves for soup, and, most surprising to me, the pear-shaped chayote that is a botanical import from Guatemala and Central America. This pale green vegetable is known as "sqoosh" (really squash) and is a valuable addition to the food chain. Walking along the winding streets or out in the countryside, the visitor spies chayote vines growing in profusion, with their green globules, the squash, hanging down.

Fresh wild mushrooms are gathered during the rainy season and sold in tidy heaps for pennies in the market. Cauliflower, eggplant, tomatoes, and bamboo shoots are plentiful. The fresh hot green chili is used now and then in the cooking of Sikkim but is not an addiction as it is in Bhutan or India.

Dairy products are important. Butter and a type of farmer's cheese are eaten daily, the cheese incorporated into soups or eaten out of hand.

Buddhist monks, Sikkim

The Sikkimese style of cooking can be characterized as simple. The people are pork-loving rice eaters, who live off the land with whatever nature provides in a mountainous region. There are few culinary surprises, but no complaints either.

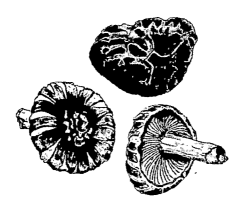

CHU-MAA
Cheese and Butter Spread

This is a nourishing, rich preparation, especially suited to mountain people, who consume a considerable amount of dairy foods and live where the temperature drops to frigid degrees as the sun descends behind the mountain ranges of the Himalayas.

2 pounds farmer's cheese
1/2 pound butter

Simmer the cheese and butter together in a pan over low heat, stirring continuously, for about 20 minutes, until the mixture is smooth and has turned a pale yellow color. Serve warm in several ways: with rice, on toast as a spread, or as an additional side dish with other Sikkimese foods. Keep, covered, in the refrigerator. Reheat gently before using.

Makes a generous 2 cups.

C H U R P I   J O H L
Cheese Soup

The first step in this tasty mountain soup is to "crack" the milk, using lemon juice, which precipitates the forming of milk solids, the curds. The whey is discarded. The soup itself can then be assembled quickly and easily and lends itself to cold winter days.

THE CHEESE

1 quart cow's milk (yak milk is used in Sikkim; see Notes)
1/2 teaspoon lemon juice

THE SOUP

1 tablespoon corn or peanut oil
1/2 teaspoon 5 phoran (5 spice; see Notes)
1 medium onion, chopped (1/2 cup)
1/2 teaspoon turmeric
1/2 cup chopped fresh tomato
1/2 teaspoon salt
The cheese derived from 1 quart milk (see above)
1 1/2 cups water

1. Bring the milk to a boil in a pan, remove it from the heat, and add the lemon juice, stirring it in. Let stand for 1–2 hours, enough time for the curds and whey to separate.
2. Pour the mixture through a piece of cheesecloth or a light kitchen towel and gently squeeze out the liquid. Discard the whey and reserve the curds (cheese) for the soup.
3. Heat the oil in a wok or pan, add the 5 phoran, and stir-fry it a few seconds. Add the onion and stir-fry for 2 minutes. Add the turmeric, tomato, salt, and cheese and stir-fry another 2 minutes.
4. Add the water, bring to a boil, and remove the pan from the heat. Do not overcook as the cheese becomes too hard. Serve hot.

Serves 4.

NOTES: There is an amusing bit of misinformation concerning the yak, which is a large bovine *(Bos grunniens),* found in the Himalayan highlands. Yak have been domesticated for their meat and milk. However, the yak is the male of the species and does not produce milk. It is the *dri,* the female, that produces the milk used by the Sikkimese to prepare this soup.

Five *phoran,* 5 spice, is a mixture of equal amounts fenugreek, mustard seed, anise seed, and two types of cuminseed. The spices are first quickly fried in a small amount of oil, as in a *baghar,* and are then ready to use.

BYASHAKHAK
Sikkimese Chicken Soup

The chickens of Sikkim were apparently especially bred to race up and down the Himalayan foothills. Picking away at the luxurious green cover on the hills, they have developed a firmness (some would say toughness) that in other countries might have come as the result of dodging cars on the roads! After long cooking this soup has the wonderfully natural flavor of these birds and proves that all that exercise was worth it.

1 pound chicken with bones, giblets, and liver included
1 medium onion, quartered (1/2 cup)
1 teaspoon salt, or to taste
4 cups water
1/4 pound dried egg noodles, 1/4 inch wide
1 chayote (see Glossary), cut into julienne strips

1. Put the chicken and chicken parts, onion, salt, and water in a pan, bring to a boil, and skim off the foam that accumulates. Cook, covered, over moderate heat for 45 minutes.
2. Add the noodles and chayote and cook for 10 minutes, which is sufficient time to tenderize them. Adjust the salt if you wish. Serve warm.

Serves 4 with other dishes.

P H I T O O
Chicken and Rice Porridge

This is a breakfast dish in Sikkim. Remember that the cold mornings at Himalayan altitudes require food that is nourishing and tasty and it has to stick to the ribs, too.

2 cups rice, rinsed and drained
1 inch fresh ginger, sliced
1 medium onion, coarsely chopped (1/2 cup)
6 cups hot water
1 cup cubed boneless chicken (1/2-inch pieces)
1 teaspoon salt, or to taste
1 tablespoon butter
1/3 cup crumbled farmer's cheese
1 teaspoon soy sauce

Put the rice, ginger, onion, water, chicken, salt, butter, and cheese in a pan and bring to a boil over moderate heat. Mix well, then simmer over low heat for 1 hour. (The rice cooks down into a thick melange. Stir in the soy sauce and cook for 5 minutes more. Serve warm.

Serves 4–6 for breakfast.

SHA-KHAK
Ground Beef Soup

The title of this recipe means "meat soup." Like so much of the cooking of Sikkim, it is direct and simple—the natural flavors of fresh mountain cooking.

1 large onion, chopped (1 cup)
2 cups water
1 scallion, green part only, chopped
1 tablespoon chopped fresh tomato
1 teaspoon finely chopped fresh ginger
1 teaspoon butter
1 teaspoon salt, or to taste
1/2 cup ground beef

Put all the ingredients together in a pan, cover, and bring to a boil over moderate heat. Cook for 10 minutes, uncover the pan, and simmer over low heat for 10 minutes more. Serve hot.

Serves 4 as a first course.

S O P S T H U
Nettle Soup with Pork

Nettle soup is the most popular soup in Sikkim. The young tops and leaves of the plant stinging nettle *(Urtica dioica L.)*, which grows to a height of three feet, are used. The plants are not cultivated but the leaves can be picked, for the asking, in the jungles surrounding the towns. The soup is slightly viscous and has a flavor somewhat like Swiss chard soup. Swiss chard is a legitimate substitute when the nettles are not available.

> *1 tablespoon corn or peanut oil*
> *1 small onion, chopped (1/4 cup)*
> *1/2 pound ground pork*
> *2 1/2 cups hot water*
> *1 pound nettle leaves (see Glossary), coarsely chopped*
> *1 teaspoon salt*

1. Heat the oil in a pan and brown the onion and pork together over moderate for 10 minutes. Add the water and bring to a boil. Add the nettle leaves and salt, cover, and cook over low heat for 15 minutes.
2. Uncover and beat the soup with a whisk for a minute to break down the leaves, but not so much as to produce a purée. The soup should have texture. Serve warm.

Serves 4.

PHAKSHA-GYARI
Pork Boil with Ginger

Pork is a popular and flavorful meat in Sikkim. The cool climate and the lush hills overgrown with ample grazing areas contribute to its popularity. Also, in a Buddhist population, pork is not a prohibited meat.

Pork prepared this way reveals its connection to a Chinese dish, and yet it is Sikkimese in origin. The meat can be served cold the next day and makes an admirable sandwich in the Western fashion.

2 *pounds boneless pork, preferably with skin*
4 *cups water*
1 *medium onion, quartered*
1 *large, fresh tomato (1/2 pound), quartered*
1 *inch fresh ginger, sliced*
1 *teaspoon salt*
1/2 *teaspoon sugar*
2 *tablespoons light soy sauce*

Put all the ingredients in a pan, bring to a boil over moderate heat, and cook, covered, for about 1 1/2 hours, or until the meat is tender. Should the liquid evaporate too quickly, add another 1/2 cup water. There is usually little sauce remaining. Cut the pork into generous slices and serve warm with or without the sauce.

Serves 6 with other dishes.

SUNGUR KO TARKAREE

Rich Pork Curry

Pork is very popular in Sikkim and relatively inexpensive. There are no dietary restrictions on eating pork by the large Buddhist community in spite of the historical knowledge that the Buddha died in the sixth century B.C. after eating what was probably tainted pork.

2 tablespoons corn or peanut oil
1 medium onion, chopped (1/2 cup)
2 teaspoons ground cumin
2 teaspoons ground coriander
1–2 teaspoons red dry chili flakes, to taste
6 cloves garlic, ground to a paste
1 inch fresh ginger, ground to a paste
1/2 teaspoon turmeric
2 cups water
2 pounds boneless pork, cut into 1 1/2-inch cubes
1 cup chopped fresh tomato
1 teaspoon salt, or to taste

1. Heat the oil in a pan, add the onion, and stir-fry over moderate heat to a rich brown color, about 4 minutes.
2. Mix the cumin, coriander, chili, garlic, ginger, and turmeric together with 2 tablespoons of the water and add it all at once to the onion mixture. Stir-fry for 3 minutes.
3. Add the pork and stir-fry for 10 minutes. Add the remaining water, tomato, and salt and cook, covered, over low heat for 1 hour, or until the pork is tender. This curry should have ample thick sauce. Serve warm with chutney, rice, and *dal* (the lentil purée) (page 49).

Serves 6.

SHYKOM
Dried Pork Sauté

Traditionally strips of pork were hung in the cool mountain air for two days, which dehydrates the meat to some extent and adds another texture when the pork is cooked. I have improvised this in New York by drying the pork on a cake rack in front of an open kitchen window on a cold evening. During the day, I put the cut of pork, uncovered, in the refrigerator and turn it over several times. This also has a drying effect.

> 3 tablespoons corn or peanut oil
> 1 large onion, chopped (1 cup)
> 1 cup chopped fresh tomato, or canned
> 2 or 3 fresh hot green chilis, to taste, chopped
> 1 teaspoon salt
> 2 pounds air-dried pork, cut into 1-inch cubes
> 1 cup water

1. Heat the oil in a pan, add the onion, tomato, chilis, and salt and stir-fry over moderate heat for 5 minutes.
2. Add the pork cubes and stir-fry for 5 minutes. Add the water, cover the pan, and cook until the pork is tender, about 45 minutes. Should the sauté seem too dry, add another 1/2 cup water. (The sauté does not have a sauce and relies on the onion and tomato to provide additional texture.) Serve warm with several other Sikkimese dishes.

Serves 6.

YUNGTSHU
PHAKSHA
Pork and Greens

Mustard greens are traditionally used in this recipe and are available in Chinese or Indian green grocers. However, Swiss chard (leaves only) could be substituted as it resembles one of the various types of garden greens grown and eaten in Sikkim.

1 tablespoon *corn or peanut oil*
1/2 *pound* Phaksha-Gyari *(page 204), cut into 1-inch cubes*
1 *small onion, coarsely chopped (1/3 cup)*
1/4 *teaspoon turmeric*
1 *pound Swiss chard leaves or mustard greens, shredded*
1 *teaspoon salt*

Heat the oil in a skillet or wok and stir-fry the pork, onion, and turmeric over moderate heat for 3 minutes to lightly brown. Add the greens and salt and stir-fry for 5 minutes longer. Serve warm.

Serves 4 with other dishes.

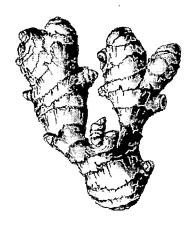

TSAP SYA NGO TSHUM
Ground Beef Fry

Pork is a most popular meat in Sikkim and this dry stir fry has many followers on account of its simplicity and flavor. I've substituted ground beef, which also has its aficionados.

2 tablespoons corn or peanut oil
1 large onion, chopped (1 cup)
1/2 teaspoon turmeric
2 teaspoons chopped fresh ginger
1 cup chopped fresh tomato, or canned
1 pound ground beef
1 teaspoon salt, or to taste

1. Heat the oil in a skillet and brown the onion and turmeric over moderate heat for 3 minutes. Add the ginger and tomato and stir-fry for 5 minutes.
2. Add the beef and salt and continue to stir-fry for 5 minutes more to cook the meat and almost completely evaporate the liquid that has accumulated. (Should you prefer to substitute ground pork, fry it an additional 5 minutes.) Serve warm with rice.

Serves 4 with other dishes.

J O O M A
Beef and Rice Sausage

Every culture that I have ever researched prepares sausage—large or small. The Sikkimese like their sausage laced with green hot chili and ginger and held together by a generous amount of cooked rice.

1 pound beef chuck, cut into 1/4-inch dice
3 cups cooked rice
1 medium onion, chopped (1/2 cup)
1 teaspoon finely chopped fresh ginger
2–3 fresh hot green chilis, to taste, chopped
1 teaspoon salt
1 yard beef sausage casing, halved crosswise

1. Mix together well the beef, rice, onion, ginger, chilis, and salt. Stuff into the sausage skins. Tie one end up tightly and leave 3 inches of the other end unfilled but tie it closed. (This space allows for the sausage to expand.)

2. Put the 2 sausages in boiling water to cover and cook over moderate heat for 1 hour. Remove from the water, cool, and refrigerate.

   To serve, slice for sandwiches and snacks, both hot and cold. My choice is to cut the sausage into 1/4-inch-thick diagonal slices and brown them in a small amount of oil and 1/4 cup thinly sliced onions.

   Should you prefer not to stuff the sausage casing, then prepare patties 3 inches in diameter and 1/2 inch thick. Press firmly together and brown in oil for 3 minutes. Drain briefly on paper towels and serve warm.

Makes enough sausage or patties for 10.

BYA TSHONYO
Rice, Beef, and Greens

When I learned how to make this dish in Sikkim, we used a green jungle leaf shaped like a nasturtium leaf. The leaves had the texture of spinach or watercress, which are easily obtainable substitutes. Only the leaves were used; the stems were discarded. This is filling mountain food for cold mornings.

1 cup rice, rinsed and drained
4 cups hot water
1/2 cup ground beef
1 teaspoon salt, or to taste
1 small onion, chopped (1/3 cup)
2 cups loosely packed spinach or watercress, coarsely shredded
1 tablespoon butter

Put all the ingredients in a pan, bring to a boil, and cook, covered, over low heat for about 45 minutes. (The rice will become soft without melting down into a smooth porridge. The color will be an attractive green.) Serve warm, with chutney.

Serves 4.

L E Y - P O
Brain Sauté

1 pound beef or lamb brain, rinsed well in cold water
1 tablespoon corn or peanut oil
1 small onion, chopped (1/3 cup)
1/4 teaspoon turmeric
1/2 teaspoon salt
2 tablespoons chopped fresh tomato, or canned
1/4 cup water

1. Put the brain in a pan, cover with hot water, and bring to a boil. Cover the pan and cook over moderate heat for 15 minutes. Remove the brain, cool, and pull off all the membranes. Cut into 1-inch cubes.
2. Heat the oil in a pan or skillet and fry the onion and turmeric over moderate heat for 2 minutes. Add the salt and tomato and stir-fry another minute.
3. Add the brain and water, cover the pan, and cook over low heat for 10 minutes to integrate the flavors. Serve warm with rice.

Serves 4 with other dishes.

NOSHYA GYARI
Top-of-the-Stove Beef Roast

The Sikkimese do not have ovens in their homes to bake food. So, here is a pot roast that cooks on top of the stove, which might have wood or kerosene as the heating element. Since the beef is tough, it's just as well that it takes twice the time to become tender as it does for meat in the United States, for example. Fresh ginger is the important flavor.

2 tablespoons corn or peanut oil
1 medium onion, chopped (1/2 cup)
1 inch fresh ginger, sliced
1/2 cup chopped fresh tomato, or canned
2 pounds boneless beef chuck, in 1 piece
2 cups water
1 teaspoon salt

1. Heat the oil in a pan, add the onion, and ginger and stir-fry over moderate heat for 2 minutes. Add the tomato and continue to stir-fry, tossing well.
2. Add the beef and brown for 5 minutes on each side. Add the water and salt and cook, covered, until the beef is tender, about 1 1/2 hours. Should the liquid evaporate too quickly, add another 1/2 cup hot water. There should be little sauce left, just enough to moisten when the meat is tender. Slice and serve warm.

Serves 6 with other dishes.

BYASHA CHUM
Chicken Curry

Chicken is the expensive meat of Gangtok, Sikkim's capital, and so it is not eaten frequently. Scallions are a popular green and are used in this case instead of the ubiquitous onion, giving a particularly fresh flavor.

The word "curry" is a catch-all phrase in Sikkim. Curry is, after all, a stew, so it becomes easy to use the word "curry" to cover any number of different preparations.

A 2-pound chicken, cut into 6 serving pieces, including giblets, or an equal number of chicken parts

4 scallions, sliced 1/4 inch thick

1 inch fresh ginger, smashed with the flat side of a cleaver

1/2 teaspoon salt, or to taste

1 tablespoon butter (optional, but traditional)

1 cup hot water

Put all the ingredients in a pan, cover, and cook over moderate/low heat until the chicken is tender, about 45 minutes. If the liquid evaporates too quickly, add another 1/2 cup water. There should be some sauce. Serve warm.

Serves 4 with other dishes.

BATAK SYA CHUM
Duck Curry

Duck is my favorite type of poultry and during my first trip to Sikkim I noticed ducks wandering around the gardens in Gangtok. Later I learned that the ducks are raised more for their eggs than for their meat, which is expensive. With their firm flesh, they are generally prepared in a long-cooking curry.

   3 *tablespoons corn or peanut oil*
   1 *medium onion, chopped (1/2 cup)*
1/2 *teaspoon turmeric*
     A 4-pound duck, cut into 8 pieces, including the giblets
   1 *teaspoon salt, or to taste*
   1 *cup chopped fresh tomato, or canned*
1 or 2 *hot green chilis, to taste, halved lengthwise*
   3 *cups water*
   1 *tablespoon chopped fresh coriander (Chinese parsley)*

1. Heat the oil in a pan, add the onion and turmeric, and stir-fry over moderate heat for 2 minutes. Add the duck pieces and brown them for 10 minutes.
2. Add the salt, tomato, and chilis and stir-fry a minute. Add the water, cover the pan, and cook over low heat until the duck is tender and the sauce thickened, about 1 1/2 hours. Should the liquid evaporate too quickly, add 1/2 cup water. Serve warm garnished with the coriander.

Serves 6 with Millet Pancakes (see page 215) and rice, if you wish.

MINCHA KHU
Millet Pancakes

Millet is a staple grain that grows well in the Himalayan altitudes of Sikkim and has been grown in Asia since prehistoric times. Should you not be able to find millet flour, the grain (used in birdseed) is often available and this can be ground to a flour in a food processor.

1 *cup millet flour*
3/4 *cup water*
1/4 *teaspoon salt*
   Peanut or corn oil for pan-frying

1. Mix the flour, water, and salt together to form a soft combination the consistency of pancake batter.
2. Heat 2 teaspoons oil in a skillet (I prefer a Teflon skillet), pour in 1/4 cup of the batter, and cook the pancake over moderate heat until browned on both sides. Make pancakes with the remaining batter in the same manner. Serve warm with any kind of Sikkimese curry.

Makes 4 to 6 pancakes.

NYA-PATSHO
Fish Cooked in Bamboo

A piece of green bamboo about twelve to fourteen inches long and five inches wide, cut from one of the bamboo trees that cover the mountains near Gangtok, is the ideal container for this recipe. The end nodule of the bamboo can be considered the bottom, while the opening is stuffed with green bamboo leaves to seal it. Green bamboo does not burn and provides the moisture with which to roast the ingredients inside the container. Traditionally, the bamboo is baked over a charcoal brazier. Cooking in bamboo must be the most primitive (earliest) method of cooking food in Sikkim. The only other region I have encountered food cooked this way is on the island of Sulawesi (Indonesia) in the land of the Toraja, where this ancient method still prevails.

With a nod to the twentieth century, the fish and seasonings here may also be wrapped in aluminum foil and baked in a 375 degree oven for 30 minutes. The fresh, green aroma of the bamboo is missing, but the result is admirable. The ideal freshwater fish is trout.

1 medium onion, sliced (1/2 cup)
1/2 inch fresh ginger, sliced
1 small hot green chili, halved
1 tablespoon soy sauce
1/2 teaspoon salt
1 pound whole freshwater fish, river or lake, cleaned
1 green bamboo container (see above)

1. Mix all the seasonings together and rub them over the inside and outside of the fish. Stuff the fish into the bamboo and close up the opening with folded bamboo leaves, banana leaves, or aluminum foil.
2. Roast the bamboo over charcoal for 30 minutes, turning it every now and then to cook evenly. Serve warm by cutting the bamboo container in half lengthwise.

Serves 4 with other dishes.

L O O P H E T A C H A R
Apple Paste Chutney

The amount of hot green chili here should be to taste, according to one's tolerance. There should be a sting to the chutney, but the apple flavor must be pronounced.

1 firm tart apple, peeled, cored, and coarsely chopped
2 tablespoons chopped onion
2 tablespoons chopped fresh tomato
1/2 teaspoon salt
1/2 teaspoon sugar
1–2 teaspoons sliced hot green chili

Grind all the ingredients to a relatively smooth paste in a food processor. Serve at room temperature with any kind of Sikkimese food.

Makes about 1 cup.

HOOSE ACHAR
Hot Green Chutney

Scallion, coriander, and hot green chili give this flavorful chutney an attractive green tinge as well as a dynamic punch—as much as you can stand.

2 *scallions, sliced*

3 *tablespoons chopped fresh coriander (Chinese parsley)*

1/2 *teaspoon chopped fresh ginger*

1/2–1 *teaspoon sliced seeded hot green chili*

Process all the ingredients together to a smooth paste. Serve at room temperature with any kind of Sikkimese or Indian foods.

Makes about 1/2 cup.

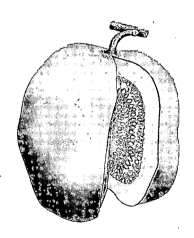

A C H A R
Table Chutney

Here is a simple daily chutney to be served any time to galvanize the tastebuds.

1 pound (2 or 3) fresh tomatoes
1–2 teaspoons dried hot red chilis, to taste
1 teaspoon salt
1 teaspoon fresh lemon juice

1. Char the skins on the tomatoes over charcoal coals or under a gas or electric broiler. Peel and discard the skins, and quarter the tomatoes.
2. Process the chilis and salt together until finely ground. Add the tomatoes and lemon juice and process to a relatively smooth paste. Serve with any kind of Sikkimese food.

Makes about 2 cups.

TOMATO ACHAR
Cooked Tomato Chutney

1 tablespoon corn or mustard oil
1 pound onions, sliced thin
1/2 inch fresh ginger, cut into very thin shreds
1 pound fresh tomatoes, sliced
1/2 teaspoon salt
1/8 teaspoon turmeric
3 small fresh hot green chilis, with a 1-inch gash cut in each
1/4 cup chopped fresh coriander (Chinese parsley)

Heat the oil in a wok or skillet, add the onions and ginger and stir-fry over moderate heat for 1/2 minute. Add the tomatoes, salt, turmeric, chilis, and coriander and stir-fry for 3 minutes. Do not overcook; this is a firm chutney. Cool, then serve at room temperature. May be refrigerated for up to 3 days. Serve with any kind of food.

Makes about 3 cups.

CHU PATSHA-DONG
Bamboo Shoots and Farmer's Cheese

The Sikkimese are dairy-oriented, with homemade fresh cheese and butter leading the way. This recipe combines them with the other Sikkimese daily food, bamboo shoots. Stands of bamboo are a common sight in the countryside around Gangtok, the capital city, where I spent some time. All bamboo may be edible but not all of it is palatable. In Sikkim, the slender cane bamboo is popular as well as the thick, meaty variety.

I learned this recipe using fresh bamboo, which is first peeled, then shaved into thin shreds with a sharp knife. The shreds are then soaked in cold water for an hour to remove their slightly bitter taste and drained. After that, the shoots are ready to use. Since fresh bamboo shoots are difficult to find, the canned type can be substituted.

3 *tablespoons butter*
1 *small onion, chopped (1/3 cup)*
1/4 *teaspoon turmeric*
1/2 *teaspoon salt*
1/2 *pound bamboo shoots, coarsely shredded*
1/2 *cup chopped fresh tomato, or canned*
1/2 *pound farmer's cheese, broken up*

Heat the butter in a pan, add the onion, turmeric, and salt, and stir-fry over moderate heat for 1 minute. Add the bamboo shoots and stir-fry for 2 minutes. Add the tomato, stir-fry for 2 minutes, and add lastly the cheese. Cook over low heat for 5 minutes. The dish should have a creamy consistency. Serve warm with bread or rice.

Serves 4.

METOK PETSHE TSHUM
Cauliflower Stir Fry

Cauliflower is a popular, available vegetable in the Himalayan regions, which include Sikkim. This simple preparation is typical of Sikkimese cooking, demonstrating how to deal with a vegetable without the long list of spices so often found in Indian recipes.

1 tablespoon corn or peanut oil
1 small onion, chopped (1/3 cup)
1/2 teaspoon turmeric
1/2 pound cauliflower, cut into 1-inch florets
1/2 cup chopped fresh tomato, or canned
1/2 teaspoon salt, or to taste

1. Heat the oil in a skillet or pan. Add the onion and turmeric and stir-fry over moderate heat for 3 minutes. The onion should be brown but not crisp.
2. Add the cauliflower, tomato, and salt and stir-fry for 2 minutes. Cover the pan and cook over low heat for 10 minutes more. Serve warm.

Serves 4 with other dishes.

DOLOM CHUM
Eggplant Curry

The long, slender Asian eggplant is meatier than its supermarket oval, bulbous cousin. I found Asian eggplant, with their intense purple skin and pronounced flavour, in the markets of Sikkim.

1 tablespoon corn or peanut oil
4 scallions, sliced 1/4 inch thick
1 pound long Asian eggplant, sliced on the diagonal 1/4 inch thick
1/2 teaspoon salt
1/3 cup chopped fresh tomato, or canned
1 teaspoon finely chopped fresh ginger
2 tablespoons chopped fresh coriander (Chinese parsley) for garnish

Heat the oil in a skillet, add the scallions, and stir-fry over moderate heat for 1 minute. Add the eggplant, salt, tomato, and ginger and continue to stir-fry 5 minutes more. Serve warm garnished with the coriander.

Serves 4 with other dishes.

NAKTEP SHYAMO
Jungle Tree Ears

Tree ears, a black fungi (*Auricularia polytricha*), are collected in the jungle and dried in the sun. They are most often used in Chinese cooking. They have a firm crunchy texture and act as an adjunct to a meal rather than as a principal component.

2 cups dried tree ears (see Glossary)
3 tablespoons butter or peanut oil
1 medium onion, chopped (1/2 cup)
1/2 cup chopped fresh tomato, or canned
1/2 teaspoon salt, or to taste
1 teaspoon chopped fresh hot green chili, or more to taste

1. Soak the tree ears in warm water to cover for 1 hour, moving them around with your fingers to remove any sand. Drain well and coarsely chop.
2. Heat the butter or oil in a skillet and lightly brown the onion over moderate heat for about 3 minutes. Add the tree ears and stir-fry for 2 minutes.
3. Add the tomato, salt, and chili and stir-fry for 5 minutes more. Serve warm with plain rice.

Serves 6 with other dishes.

S H Y A M O
Buttered Wild Mushrooms with
Onion and Hot Chilis

During the rainy season (May to October) in Sikkim, the lush Himalayan hills are filled with wild mushrooms, which are gathered for home use. One can see small heaps of them for sale in the vegetable markets. They are plentiful, popular, and selected with a judicious eye to prevent poisoning. This particular preparation was a favorite of the chogyal, the last king of Sikkim, according to his cook, Puchung Lepcha.

1/4 pound fresh homemade butter
1 pound fresh wild or cultivated mushrooms, sliced not too thin
1 small onion, sliced into rounds (1/2 cup)
1 teaspoon salt
2–4 fresh hot green chilis, to taste, halved

Melt the butter in a skillet or wok over moderate heat. Add all the ingredients at once and stir-fry for 10 minutes. Serve warm with plain rice.

Serves 6 with other dishes.

CHU LABUB
White Radish Salad

Chu labub may be considered a table chutney or a salad side dish to serve with a full meal. The Sikkimese use fresh cheese as we would mayonnaise to bind the chutney together. Since their cheese is richer, with more butterfat than ours, I have enriched this by stirring in sour cream. Although an optional choice, the sour cream addition brings this nearer to the taste of the traditional dish.

1/2 pound Chinese white radish (daikon), sliced into julienne strips
1 scallion, thinly sliced
2 tablespoons thinly sliced fresh coriander (Chinese parsley)
1/2 teaspoon salt
1/2 cup coarsely chopped fresh tomato, or canned
1/3 cup crumbled farmer's cheese mixed with 1 tablespoon sour cream
2 fresh hot green chilis, or to taste, chopped (optional)

Mix everything together and toss several times. Serve at room temperature.

Serves 4.

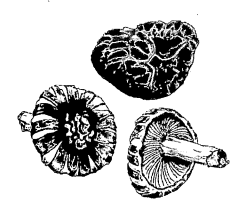

MINCHYA CHANG
Millet Beer

I'm including this recipe for historical purposes. This is the national drink of Sikkim—homemade liquor at its simplest. There is a little alcoholic content to the beer, depending upon how long the fermentation is. The more, the merrier.

20 *pounds whole millet seed*
  Cold water to cover the seed
15 *grams dry Sikkimese yeast*

1. In a large pan cover the seed with cold water, bring to a boil, and drain immediately. Toss the seed back and forth to dry somewhat.
2. Mix the millet seed with the yeast. (This should be Sikkimese yeast, prepared from natural ingredients in Sikkim.) Put the mixture in a pottery or glass jar for 2–3 days—how long will depend upon the season and the warmth of the days. An aroma will rise indicating fermentation is taking place.
3. Transfer to another container and the millet beer is ready to drink.
    The beer is served in a *toom*, a bamboo container 8 inches high and about 5 inches in diameter. The bottom nodule of the green bamboo is closed and the top nodule has been knocked out.
4. To serve, put about 3 cups of the fermented millet seed into the bamboo *toom* and pour 2 cups of hot water into the *toom*, or enough to reach the top of the container. Let stand for 10 minutes.
    Prepare a bamboo straw open on both ends and about 1/4 inch in diameter. Put the straw into the millet beer and drink heartily. (A standard straw will work just as well, too.)

⚛ 8 ⚛

FRONTIER COOKING FROM KASHMIR

If there is paradise on Earth, this is it. Oh, this is it.
— Jahangir
(Moghul Emperor, 1569–1627)

KASHMIR IS that fabled landlocked land in northwest India often equated with beauty, romance, and historical invasions. It is the area known as the Vale of Kashmir, an enclave at 5,300 feet altitude in a fertile basin surrounded by twelve- to sixteen-thousand-foot-high Himalayan Mountains. The spectacular physical beauty and grand vistas of snow-covered mountains have also produced a rich agricul-

Riverfront, Srinagar, Kashmir

Vegetable and fruit vendors, Kashmir

ture that, in turn, has created one of the richest cuisines on the Indian subcontinent.

Invaders into India about 1500 B.C. pushed their way through the natural geographical funnels of the Khyber Pass from Afghanistan into what is now Pakistan. They came from Persia, speaking an Indo-European language with a strong Caucasian connection that produced a tall people with fair skin and frequently with blue eyes. The assimilative nature of Indian civilizations and communities absorbed the invaders into the present-day people of Kashmir.

The capital city of Kashmir, Srinagar, was founded by the Hindus in the third century B.C. on Dal Lake and it ultimately established the characteristics of the region. Rice became the basic grain and yields were high in the fertile soil blessed by a congenial climate and ample water from the melting snows of the surrounding mountains.

But it was the founding of the Moghul Empire, which lasted from 1526 to 1857, by Turkic tribes that swooped in from Central Asia that produced one of India's most extraordinary civilizations, exemplified by spectacular architectural masterpieces such as the Taj Mahal. And, it was the Moghuls who established the grand cuisine that was an amalgamation of the culinary ideas brought with them from

Persia and Central Asia, which they married with the spices and seasonings they found in India. The result? Extravagant foods served in beautiful surroundings.

Kashmir has the highest protein intake of any region in India. The cool invigorating high-altitude climate invites a large consumption of meat, which is cheap and easily available there. And when one mentions meat, it means lamb or mutton. Since the population, which was initially Hindu and later Muslim, did not eat pork, the basis of the diet is lamb.

Yoghurt is used often in the cooking and is included frequently to produce rich sauces. Chicken, duck, eggs, milk, and fish from the lakes and rivers are the daily foods. *Panir,* the firm white cheese found all over India, is used in many ways in the cooking. Fruit grows in profusion and nuts, such as cashews and almonds, are ground and enrich the sauces.

It is the spices, however, that characterize Kashmir's frontier cooking with its intensely flavored meats and vegetables. The highly educated palates of the Moghuls influenced the artistic palette of the cooks at the royal level, which ultimately found its way into the kitchens of the general public. Spices like green and black cardamom pods, cinnamon in sticks and ground, fennel seeds, cloves, cumin, coriander, pepper, dried and fresh onion, ginger, garlic, the hot red chili as well as fresh red and green chilis, and turmeric are the most popular spices and seasonings. But the more esoteric *ajowan,* asafoetida, fenugreek, saffron, black salt, mustard seed, or any other ones that provided a tantalizing flavor or were noted for their medicinal efficacy were also incorporated into the cooking.

It is this insatiable search for new culinary experiences provided by the lengthy gamut of spices within a rich agricultural heritage that has resulted in the cooking of Kashmir being one of India's most outstanding cuisines.

MURGH KA KALEGI
Grilled Chicken Liver Kebabs

Here is another way that the Kashmiris prepare chicken livers when they are not including them in curries or other traditional fare. For those who enjoy the flavor and texture of chicken livers, these kebabs can be served as either an appetizer or as an additional dish on a dinner menu.

4 *cloves garlic, sliced*
1 *inch fresh ginger, sliced*
1/4 *teaspoon* garam masala (*see Glossary*)
2 *teaspoons ground coriander*
1/4 *teaspoon hot red chili powder*
1 *tablespoon lemon juice*
1/2 *cup yoghurt*
1 *teaspoon salt, or to taste*
1 *tablespoon honey*
1 *pound chicken livers, divided into lobes*
Short metal skewers, each about 6 inches long

1. In a food processor process all the ingredients together, except the livers, to a smooth paste. Marinate the chicken livers in the spice paste for 1 hour.
2. Fit 4 or 5 pieces of liver on each metal skewer. Barbecue over charcoal or under a gas or electric broiler for 5 minutes, or more should you prefer well-done s. Serve warm with mint sauce.

Serves 6 as an appetizer.

PHAY KA KABOB
Fried Fresh Lotus Snacks

The lakes of Kashmir are filled with lotus and the edible root (rhizomes). Pulling them out of the lake from the side of a small tilting canoe is sometimes arduous and back-breaking. The roots are filled with mud and must be rinsed briskly with cold water several times before use. Here is one way to prepare them. Fresh, cleaned lotus roots can be purchased during the year in New York's Chinatown.

1 *foot-long fresh lotus root, well rinsed and grated*
1 *potato, peeled and grated (1 cup)*
1 *firm unripe green banana, peeled and grated (1 cup)*
2 *tablespoons* besan *(chick-pea flour)*
1 *tablespoon pomegranate concentrate (available in Middle Eastern markets)*
1 *teaspoon chopped hot green chili*
1/2 *teaspoon salt, or to taste*
  Corn oil for deep-frying

Mix all the grated ingredients together, then add all the remaining ingredients, except the oil. Form balls 1 inch in diameter. Makes 24 balls. Heat the oil until hot in a skillet or wok and brown the balls, a few at a time, over moderate/low heat for 3 minutes. Drain on paper towels. Serves as an appetizer with Mint and Coriander Chutney (page 279).

Serves 6.

RAJMA KOFTA
Red Kidney Bean Snack

Red kidney beans are not often found in Indian cooking but they are in Kashmir—as in this tasty appetizer. High in protein and seasoned with traditional Kashmiri spices, this *kofta* has both texture and bite.

1 cup dried red kidney beans, soaked overnight in water and drained
1/2 cup chopped onion
1 teaspoon chopped fresh hot green chili
1 tablespoon chopped fresh coriander (Chinese parsley)
1 teaspoon cuminseed
1/4 teaspoon coriander seed
4 cloves garlic, chopped
1/2 inch fresh ginger, chopped
1 teaspoon salt, or to taste
1 teaspoon pomegranate concentrate (available in Middle Eastern markets)
Corn oil for deep-frying

1. Cook the beans in 3 cups water for 10 minutes. (This will loosen their skins.) Drain and pull off the outer skins. The inner pulp will still have some firmness to it.
2. In a food processor process the bean pulp with all the ingredients, except the oil. Shape the mixture into balls about 1/2 inch in diameter.
3. In a pan heat the oil until hot over moderate/low heat, add the balls, a few a time, and brown them for about 5 minutes, or until crisp. Drain on paper towels. Serve as an appetizer with mint sauce.

Makes 12 balls.

POLACK DAL KA SHORBA
Spinach and Lentil Soup

Frontier cooking does not have many vegetarian dishes since most of the frontier people are distinctly meat-eaters. They require the protein in meat and have a ready supply of goats and sheep to satisfy their needs. This soup, completely vegetarian, is eaten all over India. It is nutritious, filling, and satisfying in every way. The hallmark of good vegetarian cooking is that one never notices the absence of meat, and you don't in this soup.

1 tablespoon corn oil
1 inch fresh ginger, chopped
3 cloves garlic, chopped
1 small onion, chopped (1/2 cup)
1/4 teaspoon cuminseed
1/8 teaspoon hing (asafoetida; see Glossary)
1 teaspoon salt, or to taste
1 ripe medium tomato, chopped (1/2 cup)
1 pound fresh spinach, well rinsed in cold water
1/2 cup red lentils, covered in water and cooked until tender (see Note)
1/2 cup dried yellow split peas, covered in water and cooked until tender
1 cup milk
4 cups water
Lemon wedges and fresh coriander sprigs (Chinese parsley) for garnish

Heat the oil in a pan and sauté the ginger, garlic, onion, and cuminseed over low heat for 2 minutes. Add the *hing*, salt, tomato, spinach, and cooked lentils and split peas, milk, and water. Simmer over low heat for 20 minutes. Process the mixture in a food processor until smooth. Serve warm garnished with lemon wedges and coriander sprigs.

Serves 6.

NOTE: Cook the lentils and split peas until tender in separate saucepans. Do not cook them together, as one ingredient.

ZAKHANI SHORBA
Spiced Bone Soup

The winter months are frigid in the mountainous frontier regions. I did some traveling on horseback in the upper hills of Kashmir on a path just wide enough for the horses to pass through; the snow was piled about eight feet on each side. Overhead the sun burned in a flawlessly blue sky. The tough frontier people enjoy days with weather like that and, in fact, require this soup to fight off the all-pervasive chill.

Zakhani is an Urdu/Persian word that can be translated as soup prepared from the bones of goats. The *seena*, the breast of the goat (or lamb), is the part of the animal used.

2 *pounds goat (or lamb) bones and breast meat* (seena), *trimmed of fat and the meat cut into 1-inch cubes*
1 *inch fresh ginger, sliced*
6 *cloves garlic, chopped*
1 *scallion, chopped*
6 *dried apricots*
1 *cup yoghurt*
3 *whole dried hot red chilis*
1 *teaspoon fennel seed*
1 *teaspoon salt, or to taste*
7 *cups water*
1/2 *cup Crispy Fried Onions (page 242)*

1. In a large pan combine all the ingredients, except the fried onions, bring to a boil, and skim off the foam. Cover the pan and cook over low heat for 1 1/2 hours. This should be enough time to tenderize the meat and integrate the flavors.
2. Remove and discard the bones. Serve the soup with the meat. Garnish with the fried onions.

Serves 6.

NOTE: Pregnant women are given this soup for strength during pregnancy. And after the child is born, the convalescing mother continues to be fed it for some weeks to assist her in regaining her strength.

NOORI KOFTA
Boatman's Fish Ball

This is romantic cooking from Kashmir. A boatman paddling his canoe on one of the lakes in the beautiful Vale of Kashmir fell in love with a girl called Noori. In order to declare his affection, he prepared a luscious platter of fish balls from his family recipe and presented it to her. Was this declaration effective and did they live happily ever after? Yes, since the recipe is named after his beloved Noori. Thus their romance is remembered.

 2 *pounds fresh lake fish, such as pike or whitefish, or saltwater fish, such*
  as flounder
1/2 *cup finely chopped onion*
1/2 *inch fresh ginger, chopped fine*
 3 *cloves garlic, chopped fine*
 1 *teaspoon chopped fresh hot green chili*
 1 *teaspoon salt, or to taste*
1/4 *teaspoon* garam *masala*
 2 *tablespoons softly cooked yellow split peas*
 2 *cups water*
 1 *cup yoghurt*
 1 *teaspoon fennel seed*
 1 *whole dried hot red chili*
1/2 *cup chopped fresh tomato*
 1 *tablespoon corn oil*
 1 *tablespoon chopped fresh coriander (Chinese parsley) for garnish*

1. In a food processor process together the fish, onion, ginger, garlic, green chili, salt, *garam masala*, and split peas. With the mixture form balls about 1 1/2 inches in diameter. Makes 12 fish balls.
2. Put the water in a pan or skillet and bring to a boil. Add the balls, 1 at a time, and cook over moderate heat for 5 minutes. Remove the balls.
3. To the broth in the pan add the yoghurt, fennel seed, whole

red chili, tomato, and oil. Simmer, uncovered, over low heat for 15 minutes.
4. Return the fish balls to the sauce and cook for 5 minutes more. Serve warm garnished with the fresh coriander.

Serves 6 with pilau.

MAHAI KEBAB
Boatman's Fresh Fish Barbecue

The Vale of Kashmir with its glorious lakes and Himalayan vistas is no longer what it once was. I visited there several times before politics reared its ugly head and saw it during what some Kashmiris refer to as its golden age.

I moved into a houseboat and bought my trinkets and real saffron gathered in the hills from the Suffering Moses shop. Plying the waters of Dal Lake were boatmen in their canoes laden with flowers, wood, or anything else that they could sell. Prominently visible in each boat was the *chula*, a small charcoal brazier, on which the boatmen barbecued this dish.

A 2-pound freshwater fish, such as perch, pike, or carp, or an equal amount of saltwater fish
1 *teaspoon turmeric*
1 *teaspoon hot red chili powder*
1/4 *teaspoon* ajowan *(see Glossary)*
1 *teaspoon salt, or to taste*
1/4 *teaspoon* hing *(asafoetida; see Glossary)*
1 *tablespoon lemon juice*
4 *cloves garlic*
1 *teaspoon chopped fresh mint*

1. Clean the whole fish well, including the head and tail. Skewer the fish from stem to stern with either a metal or bamboo rod. (The Kashmiris use bamboo.)
2. In a food processor process all the remaining ingredients to a smooth paste with 2 tablespoons water. Rub the spice paste all over the fish and let stand 15 minutes. Barbecue the fish over charcoal or under a gas or electric broiler for about 10 minutes, turning the fish several times during cooking.

Serves 6 as an appetizer or as a main course.

KERAI MUCHLI
Tamarind Fish in a *Kerai*

A *kerai* is an Indian version of the round-bottomed Chinese wok and an indispensable kitchen utensil for rich and poor alike. The characteristic flavor of tamarind is popular in many tropical countries in both Asia and Central America. If unavailable, in this recipe only substitute one tablespoon pomegranate concentrate, which is available in Middle Eastern markets.

1 cup chopped onion
1 inch fresh ginger, chopped
6 cloves garlic, chopped
1 teaspoon caraway seed
1/16 teaspoon hing (asafoetida; see Glossary)
4 whole dried hot red chilis
1 teaspoon turmeric
1 teaspoon salt
1 1/2 cups water
3 tablespoons corn oil
1 tablespoon tamarind paste soaked in 1/2 cup water, strained through a metal sieve, seeds and fibres discarded
1/2 cup chopped ripe tomato
2 1/2 pounds fillet of flounder, red snapper, or similar freshwater fish
1 tablespoon chopped fresh coriander (Chinese parsley)

1. In a food processor process the onion, ginger, garlic, caraway seed, *hing*, chilis, turmeric, and salt with the water.
2. Put the oil in a wok or *kerai*, add the spice paste, and brown it lightly over low heat for 5 minutes. Add the tamarind juice and tomato and simmer for 10 minutes. Add the fish slices and cook, basting occasionally, for 15 minutes. Serve warm garnished with the coriander.

Serves 6.

R I S T A
The Small Meat Ball

To prepare *rista* you use the same meat-pulverizing method as for *gustava* (page 243). When one walks along the narrow lanes of Srinagar, the capital city of Kashmir, the dull pounding noise emanating from the homes is that of either goat or lamb meat being pounded. I recommend that whichever meat you choose be finely ground in an electric grinder or food processor. Back home in Vermont, we usually ground our own beef in a hand-grinder that was screwed onto the kitchen table. That way you could control both the quality of the meat and the fineness of the grind.

Goat is sold in several sections of New York City, but especially in the Muslim *halal* meat markets.

> 3 *pounds cubed boneless young goat or lamb (shoulder and/or rib steak)*
> 1/4 *pound kidney fat, chopped (optional)*
> 1 *tablespoon chopped fresh coriander (Chinese parsley)*
> 1 *teaspoon hot red chili powder*
> 5 *cloves garlic, chopped*
> 1 *inch fresh ginger, chopped*
> 1 *teaspoon turmeric*
> 1 *tablespoon ground cumin*
> 1 *teaspoon salt, or to taste*
> 4 *tablespoons mustard or corn oil*
> 3 *cups Crispy Fried Onions (page 242)*
> 1 *cup yoghurt*
> 4 *cups stock, prepared from goat or lamb bones, strained*
> 1 *cup chopped fresh tomato*

1. In a food processor grind together the cubed meat, kidney fat, coriander, chili powder, half of the garlic and ginger, 1/2 teaspoon of the turmeric, half of the ground cumin, and the salt. Process the mixture 3 times to insure that the meat is ground fine and well mixed with the seasonings. Form 12 round balls or oval-shaped balls. Set aside.
2. Heat the oil in a pan, add the remaining garlic, ginger, turmeric, and cumin and stir-fry over low heat for 1 minute.

3. In the processor combine the crispy onions, yoghurt, stock, and tomato to a smooth liquid. Add the liquid to the garlic/ginger mixture and bring to a boil. Add the meat balls, one by one, cover the pan, and cook over low heat for 1 hour. This will reduce the sauce to a thick consistency. Serve warm with rice and bread.

Serves 6.

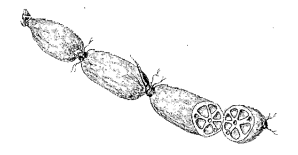

CRISPY FRIED ONIONS

1 pound small onions (about 2 inches in diameter or even smaller), peeled
Salt
Corn oil for deep-frying

1. Cut each onion in half from stem to root end. Cut each half into thin slices. Sprinkle with 2 teaspoons salt and toss well to mix. Let stand 20 minutes.
2. Put the onions in a kitchen towel and squeeze them firmly to remove as much liquid as possible.
3. Heat 1 cup oil until hot in a wok or skillet. Add the onions in batches and fry slowly over low heat so that they do not burn. Stir frequently. When the onions begin to turn brown, quickly remove them with a slotted spoon and let them drain on paper towels. They will become crispy. Store in a jar with a tight cover. Sprinkle as a garnish over any kind of rice.

Makes 1 1/2 cups.

GUSTAVA
The Big Meat Ball

Gustava is the quintessential Kashmiri dish of a certain historical era and is prepared with considerable concentration and elan. The indispensable piece of equipment for properly pulverizing the meat for the meat ball is the *mundhi*, a rectangular grinding stone, slightly concave, which holds the meat. A wood mallet of considerable heft pounds the cubes of meat in a rhythmic stroke for two hours, interrupted every now and then by a light splash of water to moisten the mixture. Sinew and tough meat fibres from the naturally grazing frontier goats are removed as they appear. At the end, the meat is soft and silky.

My cooking teacher insisted that only the boneless shoulder and rib steak of a baby goat, tender, succulent, fat-free, can produce the old-time texture and flavor of a true *Gustava*. When I mentioned using lamb, he dismissed this un-Kashmiri-like suggestion with a trace of pity. How could anyone except a foreigner suggest such a strange idea?

Nevertheless, I do recommend using boneless shoulder and rib steak of a lamb. It works very well; the texture and flavor are similar to goat and lamb is always available in supermarkets.

3 *pounds cubed boneless baby goat or lamb (shoulder and/or rib steaks)*
1/4 *pound kidney fat, chopped (optional, but traditional)*
1 *teaspoon salt, or to taste*
1 *tablespoon ground fenugreek (see Glossary)*
8 *dried hot red chilis*
1 *tablespoon chopped fresh coriander (Chinese parsley)*
3 *cups yoghurt, well beaten to prevent separation*
4 *cups goat stock, prepared from goat bones, strained*
2 *tablespoons mustard oil*
4 *whole cloves garlic*
1 *inch fresh ginger*
1 *tablespoon ground fennel, toasted*

1. Grind the boneless goat or lamb cubes and the kidney fat, if used, together in a food processor. Repeat 2 more times, for 1 minute each, to reduce to a very fine silky consistency. For the

third grinding, add the salt, fenugreek, 4 of the chilis, and the coriander. Process well to distribute the seasonings.

Using all the meat, form 2 very large meat balls. This is the traditional method. For modern use, and another method I also experienced in Kashmir, you can divide the meat and roll it into 6 equal balls.

2. Mix the yoghurt and stock together in a pan. Heat the oil in a skillet over moderate heat and stir-fry the garlic and ginger until brown. Add to the yoghurt/stock mixture. Add the remaining 4 chilis and the 2 large meat balls. Bring to a boil, cover the pan, and simmer over low heat for 2 hours. The sauce will reduce to a thick consistency and the meat balls will be soft and silky. Serve warm garnished with the toasted ground fennel.

Serves 6 with rice and bread.

NOTE: In the traditional style of dining, the diners sit around a low table or on the carpeted floor and pull at the meat balls with their fingers, helping themselves to the luxurious sauce, with rice and bread. When six meat balls are prepared, each diner enjoys one generous meat ball.

AFGHANI BARRA
KEBAB
A Wedding Barbecue: Kebab of Young Goat

The original, traditional Afghan village barbecue to celebrate weddings has spilled over into other Himalayan regions as well. It is a wild, joyous, uninhibited event, with dancing, drinking, where all are invited.

Here is how the barbecue goes: A newly completed clay platform is constructed in an outdoor area and a large charcoal fire is prepared. Slabs of young goat meat are hung over the fire and turned now and then to catch the intense heat. As the lower part of the carcass, which is closest to the fire, is roasted through, male members of the throng cut off chunks of meat and bone and triumphantly munch on the meat.

1 cup yoghurt
Juice of 1 gul-gul (see Note) or 2 tablespoons lemon juice
1 tablespoon black or regular salt
1 tablespoon finely chopped mint
Pinch nutmeg
1 tablespoon pomegranate concentrate (available at Middle Eastern markets)
5 pounds young goat ribs and shanks, cut into serving pieces

1. Mix all the ingredients together, except the meat, to make a marinade. Add the goat pieces and marinate for 1 hour.
2. Barbecue the goat over charcoal or in a gas or electric broiler over moderate/low heat for 15–20 minutes, or until tender when tested. Serve warm with mint sauce, breads, and chopped scallions.

Serves 6.

NOTE: *Gul-gul* is a large Kashmiri lemon, very likely the citron.

KABULI KOFTA
Meat Balls from Kabul

The name of this dish reveals its origin. Kabul is the capital of Afghanistan, but by using it I am also implying that this is country cooking, not necessarily confined to the city of Kabul. Frontier cooking covers a lot of territory, especially since nomads take their culinary habits with them.

The meat used can be goat, lamb, beef, or chicken, but goat and lamb are most frequently the meat of choice.

FOR THE MEAT BALLS
- 1 pound ground goat or lamb
- 1 tablespoon dried fenugreek leaves or 1 teaspoon dried fenugreek powder (see Glossary)
- 1 teaspoon ground coriander
- 1 teaspoon ground cumin
- 1 egg, beaten
- 6 dried, but soft apricots

FOR THE SAUCE
- 3 cloves garlic, smashed
- 1/2 inch fresh ginger, smashed
- 1 medium onion, chopped (1/2 cup)
- 1 fresh ripe tomato, chopped (1/3 cup)
- 1/4 teaspoon hot red chili powder
- 1/2 teaspoon paprika
- 1/2 teaspoon salt, or to taste
- 1/4 teaspoon turmeric
- 3 tablespoons corn oil
- 1 cup yoghurt, beaten
- 1 cup water

1. Prepare the meat balls: Mix all the ingredients, except the apricots. Divide the mixture into 6 equal parts and roll each part into a ball. Stuff each ball with an apricot. Roll the ball again to encase the fruit and set aside.

2. Prepare the sauce: Grind the garlic, ginger, onion, and tomato together to a paste in a food processor. Add the chili powder, paprika, salt, and turmeric and mix well.
3. Heat the oil in a large skillet, add the spice paste, and simmer over low heat for 5 minutes. Add the yoghurt and continue to cook slowly for 5 minutes. Add the water, bring to a boil, and simmer for 15 minutes.
4. Add the meat balls to the sauce, cover the pan, and simmer over low heat for 20 minutes to thicken the sauce. Serve warm with rice, breads, and chutney.

Serves 6.

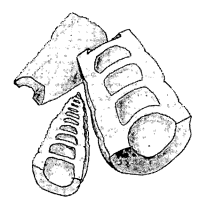

SIKANDHRI RAAN
Roast Leg of Baby Goat

When Alexander the Great's route took him toward the east, through Central Asia and northern India to Swat, in what is now Pakistan, he established his culinary ideas as well as the Greco-Buddhist style of art known as Gandhara. Frontier cooking, a crosscurrent of several cultures, has its own agenda, as this boiled, spiced, then roasted baby leg of goat demonstrates. The people of that region prefer goat since they say it does not have the penetrating aroma that sheep meat does. However, when young goat is not available, one can use leg of baby lamb.

　3　*pounds leg of young goat*
　12　*cloves garlic, chopped fine or crushed*
　4　*inches fresh ginger, chopped fine or crushed*
　1　*tablespoon crushed mint leaves*
　2　*scallions, chopped*
　4　*bay leaves*
　1　*inch cinnamon stick*
　1　*cup yoghurt*
　2　*tablespoons fresh lemon juice*
1/2　*teaspoon saffron threads*
　1　*teaspoon* garam masala *(see Glossary)*
　1　*tablespoon pomegranate concentrate (available at Middle Eastern markets)*
　1　*teaspoon salt, or to taste*

1. Cut ten 1-inch-deep slits in the goat leg all over it.
2. Put 2 quarts of water in a large pan, add the garlic, ginger, mint leaves, scallions, bay leaves, and cinnamon. Bring the water to a boil and add the goat leg. Cook over moderate heat for 1/2 hour. The heat penetrates into the meat through the slits cut in the leg. Remove the leg from the pan.
3. In a shallow dish large enough to hold the goat leg mix together the yoghurt, lemon juice, saffron, garam masala, pomegranate concentrate, and salt. Rub the yoghurt mixture into and all over the leg and let stand 15 minutes.

4. Grill the goat over charcoal or under a gas or electric broiler, turning the leg, for 20 minutes.
5. Meanwhile, reduce the yoghurt mixture in a pan over moderate heat to about 1 cup. This sauce will be served with the meat.
6. Slice the goat meat and serve warm. Pour the spice sauce over it. Serve with bread, pilau, and various chutneys.

Serves 6 or 7.

The Himalaya Mountains, Kashmir

NALLI KA NASHA
Baby Goat Shank Stew

This is an old frontier recipe, one that is eaten everywhere and especially in Kashmir, Pakistan, and the mountain regions to the north. What could be easier for nomadic people as they tend their flocks of goats and sheep in the Himalayan hills than to combine goat meat, dried fruit, yoghurt, and several seasonings in a pot over a wood fire? Although this recipe calls for goat meat, lamb is a legitimate substitution.

5 pounds baby goat shanks, meat and bone, cut into serving pieces, or lamb shanks
5 cloves garlic, chopped
1 tablespoon finely chopped peeled ginger
1 cup dried apricots
1 teaspoon salt, or more to taste
1 cup yoghurt, well beaten
5 cups water

1. Put all the ingredients in a large pan and bring to a boil. Cover and simmer over low heat for about 1 hour, or until the meat is tender. Remove the shanks to a roasting pan.
2. Reduce the liquid in the pan to 2 cups. Pour the sauce over the meat, cover the roasting pan, and bake the meat in a preheated 350 degree oven for 15 minutes. (The sauce will thicken and the meat will become crisp.) Serve warm with bread and pilau.

Serves 6.

MAGZ KA MASALA
Spiced Lamb Brains

One of my favorite foods from any culture is brain. In this Kashmiri combination, a number of very potent spices and seasonings are combined with the precooked brains. The tender, melting texture, with its assertive flavors, makes a wonderful side dish.

4	cups water
6	lamb brains
3	tablespoons corn oil
2	cups chopped onions
1	inch fresh ginger, chopped
4	cloves garlic, chopped
2 or 3	hot green chilis, chopped
1/2	teaspoon turmeric
1	teaspoon paprika
1/2	teaspoon hot red chili powder
1/2	teaspoon garam masala (see Glossary)
1	cup chopped ripe tomato
1	teaspoon salt, or to taste
5	curry leaves, fresh or dried
3	tablespoons chopped fresh coriander (Chinese parsley) for garnish

1. Bring 4 cups water to a rapid boil, add the lamb brains, and parboil over moderate heat for 5 minutes. Drain well.
2. Heat the oil in a pan. Add the onions, ginger, garlic, and green chilis and stir-fry over moderate/low heat until the onions are colored light brown.
3. Add the turmeric, paprika, chili powder, *garam masala*, tomato, salt, and curry leaves and continue to stir-fry over low heat for 10 minutes.
4. Add the brains and cook for 10 minutes more, turning the brains to coat with the spice mixture. Garnish with the coriander. Serve warm with rice, *chapatti* or *naan*.

Serves 6.

BAKRA KA CHOP
Grilled Lamb Chops, Bukhara Style

The Moghul origin of this lamb chop recipe emanated from Bukhara in Central Asia and then permeated throughout the frontier region to include Kashmir. It has become a popular dish there.

  1 tablespoon pomegranate concentrate (available in Middle Eastern markets)
    Pinch hing (asafoetida, see Glossary)
  1 teaspoon salt
  1 teaspoon cuminseed lightly toasted in a dry skillet
  2 tablespoons white vinegar
1/4 cup yoghurt
  1 teaspoon black pepper
  4 cloves garlic, sliced
  6 rib lamb chops (2 pounds)

1. In a food processor process all the ingredients together, except the lamb chops, to a paste. Marinate the chops in the spice paste for 1 hour.
2. Grill the chops over charcoal or under a gas or electric broiler for 5 minutes on each side. Serve warm with sliced cucumbers, tomatoes, and scallions and mint sauce. Pilau and *naan* bread may also be served.

Serves 6.

TABAC MAZ
Grilled Lamb Chops in Yoghurt Sauce

In Srinagar tender lamb chops are prepared with a lightly spiced yoghurt sauce. I used to walk down the dirt road in search of the yoghurt merchant who would sell his product, scooping it out from the large brown clay jugs in which it had been fermenting. When purchased straight from the horse's mouth, so to speak, the yoghurt was always clean and rich.

Although the traditional way of preparing this dish is to use the rib chops of lamb or goat, I find that the shoulder chop with bone is also luscious. Very often, it is the sauce that really counts.

2 *cups water*
2 *cups yoghurt*
3 *pounds rib or shoulder lamb or goat chops, cut into 6 pieces*
1 *teaspoon salt, or to taste*
4 *cloves garlic, chopped*
1 *inch fresh ginger*
2 *whole dried hot red chilis*
2 *cardamom pods (sometimes black cardamom is used)*
3 *bay leaves*
3 *whole cloves*
   Lemon wedges and sliced onions for serving

1. Put the water in a pan and bring it to a boil. Add the lamb chops and cook over moderate heat until soft, about 1/2 hour. Remove and set aside.
2. Add the yoghurt to the pan with the salt, garlic, ginger, chilis, cardamom pods, bay leaves, and cloves. Simmer over moderate/low heat for 20 minutes to reduce the sauce. Return the chops to the sauce and simmer over low heat for 10 minutes. Remove the chops and keep the sauce warm.
3. Grill the chops over charcoal or under a gas or electric broiler until brown. Serve warm with the yoghurt sauce, lemon wedges, sliced onions, and mint sauce.

Serves 6 with pilau and Indian breads.

BAKRA KA
PASANDA
Royal Lamb in Nut Sauce

Pasanda is an extraordinary Moghul dish enjoyed with gusto by Akbar the Great (1542–1605) during his reign. It is said that the recipe arrived with a Persian cook to the court of Akbar in the sixteenth century where it was immediately assigned a special status by Akbar, who elevated the prestige of the dish by his royal enjoyment of it.

Nowadays, *pasanda*, an essentially Muslim preparation, is expensive to produce and requires several unusual ingredients, all of them available in Indian food shops. It is one of India's greatest culinary expressions. *Pasanda* can be prepared with boneless lamb or goat steaks.

2 *tablespoons poppy seeds* (khuskhus)
2 *tablespoons dried peeled melon or pumpkin seeds*
2 *tablespoons blanched almonds*
2 *tablespoons raw cashew nuts*
5 *dried rosebuds*
1 *cup water*
1 *cup milk*
1 *cup yoghurt*
1 *teaspoon black peppercorns*
1 *teaspoon cuminseed*
4 *cardamom pods*
1 *teaspoon salt, or to taste*
3 *pounds boneless lamb or goat steaks, cut into 6 equal slices*
4 *tablespoons corn oil or* ghee *(clarified butter)*

1. Rinse the poppy seeds thoroughly several times in water to remove the impurities. Rinse the melon seeds, if using, almonds, cashews, and rosebuds in the same manner. Then cover these ingredients with 1 cup water and soak for 1 hour to soften.
2. Put the seeds, nuts, rosebuds, and water in a food processor and blend for 2 minutes to chop. Add the milk and process until smooth. Set aside.

3. In the processor process the yoghurt, peppercorns, cuminseed, cardamom pods, and salt to a smooth paste. Marinate the steaks in the paste for 1/2 hour.
4. Heat the oil or *ghee* in a pan, add the steaks and marinade, and simmer over low heat for 15 minutes. Carefully pour in the milk/nut mixture and simmer until the sauce has thickened and the steaks are tender, about 20 minutes, basting several times. Remove the steaks to a serving platter and spoon the thickened sauce over them. Serve with pilau and *naan*.

Serves 6.

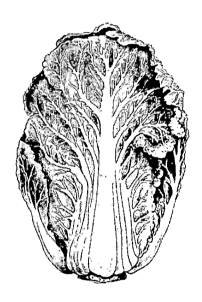

CHAPLEE KEBAB
Fat-Tailed Sheep Barbecue

One of the amusing sights, to me, anyway, was to see the sheep of the frontier region, and sometimes also in North Africa, dragging their full, round, and ponderous fat tails over the ground as they grazed. On one occasion I saw a particularly large tail that had been tied to a small cart with wheels, which allowed the sheep to move about more freely. No animal abuse there!

Geographically, the frontier region, sometimes known as the Northwest Frontier Province during the British colonial period, consisted of what is now northern Pakistan and India. But with fluid borders in that era from a culinary point of view, Afghanistan and Kashmir must be included for good measure.

In common parlance, *chaplee* is a flat, crisp hamburger.

2 1/2 pounds ground lamb (from the ribs or filet)
  1 tablespoon chopped sheep tail fat (optional, but traditional)
  1 scallion, chopped fine
  3 cloves garlic, chopped fine
  1 inch ginger, chopped fine
  1 tablespoon pomegranate concentrate (available in Middle Eastern markets)
  1/4 teaspoon garam masala
  1 tablespoon chopped fresh coriander (Chinese parsley)
  1/4 teaspoon chopped fresh mint
  1/2 teaspoon salt, or to taste
  1/4 teaspoon ground coriander
  1/4 teaspoon ground cumin
  1 tablespoon bhuna channa *or toasted* besan *(see Note)*
  1 egg, beaten

1. To make the kebab mixture, mix the ground lamb and all the remaining ingredients together until well combined. Divide the mixture into 6 equal parts and form each part into a ball. Flatten the balls into patties, each about 4 inches in diameter and 3/4 inch thick.

2. Grill the kebabs over charcoal or under a gas or electric broiler for 3 minutes on each side. (You can also pan-fry the patties in oil until well done—another cooking option.) Serve with mint chutney and Saffron Rice (page 271).

Serves 6, one generous patty per person.

NOTE: *Bhuna channa* are toasted chick-peas and can be purchased in Middle Eastern markets. I buy them from a shop in Brooklyn and they are always available. The *channa* can be eaten out of hand, like peanuts, and they're nice to serve at cocktail hour. For this recipe they must be ground into a flour.

In the event that *bhuna channa* are not available, *besan* (chick-pea flour) can be lightly toasted in a dry skillet until the aroma rises and it has turned light tan in color.

HIREAN KA ACHAR
Pickled Deer Meat

In the early days of the Moghul Empire there were enough deer roaming wild in Kashmir and the other frontier mountain regions for hunters to shoot them for sport or food. One of the popular methods of preserving the deer meat when the catch was excessive was to pickle the cubes and store them for future celebrations.

This recipe is of Moghul origin and is presented for historical purposes. This should not, however, deter you from using the process to pickle deer meat. During the legal hunting season in New England, for example, it is possible to purchase fresh deer meat.

3 *pounds boneless deer meat, cut into 2-inch cubes*
1 *cup mustard oil (more traditionally used) or corn oil (of more modern usage)*
3 *cloves garlic, chopped*
1 *inch fresh ginger, chopped*
1 *tablespoon ground fennel seed*
1 *tablespoon mustard seed*
1 *tablespoon fenugreek seed (see Glossary)*
1 *teaspoon turmeric*
1 *teaspoon salt*
1 *teaspoon hot red chili powder*
1 *tablespoon ground coriander*
1 *cup vinegar*

1. Cover the deer meat with water (5 cups or more) in a large pan, and bring to a boil. Simmer, covered, over moderate heat until *nearly* soft, about 1 hour. Drain.
2. Heat the oil until hot in a pan. Add the garlic and ginger and stir-fry them over low heat until brown. Add the fennel, mustard, fenugreek, turmeric, salt, chili powder, and coriander and stir-fry rapidly over heat for 1/2 minute. Do not burn. Add the vinegar and simmer for 5 minutes.
3. Add the deer meat and stir-fry until the mixture is completely dry except for the oil. Cool completely.

Store in a glass jar with a tight cover. The oil will rise to the top, cover the meat, and preserve it for an indefinite time—some say at least a year.

Serve cold as a snack. Be sure not to touch the ingredients in the jar with your fingers as this can contaminate the contents and produce spoilage! Use a wooden spoon to remove the pickled deer cubes.

Makes about 2 quarts.

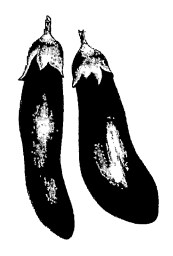

MURGH MUGHLAI
Chicken Chop

This recipe is from the time of Akbar, the great Moghul emperor of Hindustan who lived from 1542–1605. (The Moghul era itself was from 1526–1857.) Akbar was considered the greatest Moghul, having left behind great artistic and architectural monuments.

In the original, very ancient recipe the bread crumbs were prepared by pulverizing a dried *chapatti* into a smooth powder. This chicken is accompanied by chopped scallions, sprigs of fresh coriander, lemon wedges, and, surprisingly, mint sauce, as well.

1 egg, beaten
1 teaspoon salt, or to taste
1 tablespoon lemon juice
1/4 teaspoon white pepper
1 teaspoon chopped hot green chili
3 whole breasts of chicken, halved (6 pieces)
1/2 cup dry bread crumbs
1/2 cup flour
1/2 cup corn oil for pan-frying

1. Mix together the egg, salt, lemon juice, pepper, and chili. Add the chicken pieces, toss to coat, and marinate for 1/2 hour.
2. Mix the bread crumbs and flour together. Dip each chicken breast in the crumb mixture to cover completely and set aside.
3. Heat the oil until hot in a large skillet and brown the chicken over moderate-low heat on both sides for 5–7 minutes. Drain briefly on paper towels. Serve the chicken warm with chopped scallions, sprigs of fresh coriander, lemon wedges, and mint sauce.

Serves 6.

MURGH KA SEENA
Grilled Breast of Chicken Chop

Here is a frontier chicken recipe that may have originated in Afghanistan (also called the Northwest Frontier), but one that is now eaten everywhere in northern India and in those regions with Moghul influence. My cook in Calcutta used to prepare this chicken chop during my years of residence there. And I do it now in New York City when my mood turns to well-seasoned chicken that is also tender and moist.

10 *cloves garlic, chopped fine or crushed in a mortar*
  1 *inch fresh ginger, sliced and crushed in a mortar or food processor*
1/4 *teaspoon* garam masala *(see Glossary)*
  1 *cup yoghurt, beaten*
  1 *teaspoon salt, or to taste*
1/4 *teaspoon saffron threads*
  1 *tablespoon pomegranate concentrate (available in Middle Eastern markets)*
  1 *teaspoon paprika*
1/2 *teaspoon crushed fresh hot green chili*
1/2 *teaspoon chopped mint leaves*
  1 *tablespoon lemon juice*
  3 *pounds breast of chicken (8 pieces)*
    Sliced onions and lemon wedges for serving

1. The entire list of spices and seasonings may be ground together in a food processor. Then mix everything together, except the chicken.

2. Then marinate the chicken breasts, divided, in the spice sauce for a minimum of 1 hour or overnight, which will intensify the flavor and tenderize the meat. If marinating it overnight, refrigerate the mixture, covered.

2. When ready to dine, remove the chicken from the marinade and barbecue the pieces over charcoal or under a gas or electric broiler for about 7 minutes, turning the chicken once. Serve warm garnished with slices of onion and lemon wedges.

Serves 6 to 8.

MURGH ROGHNI
Chicken with Red Cheeks

Rathan joth is the Kashmiri expression that implies a healthy blush to the cheeks. Preparing this dish with paprika is designed to produce a red color in the sauce and, therefore, to the red cheeks. The interpretation is mine.

1 tablespoon paprika

4 scallions, sliced

2 tablespoons pomegranate concentrate (available in Middle Eastern markets)

5 stems of garlic scallions, sliced, or 1 clove garlic, sliced

1 teaspoon salt, or to taste

10 blanched almonds

3 tablespoons corn oil

2 1/2 pounds boneless chicken parts, breast and thighs, loose skin and fat discarded, or a 3-pound chicken, cut into 8 pieces

1 1/2 cups warm water

1. In a food processor process the paprika, scallions, pomegranate concentrate, garlic scallions, salt, and almonds with 2 tablespoons water to a smooth paste.
2. Heat the oil until hot in a skillet or pan and sauté the spice paste over low heat for 5 minutes.
3. Add the chicken pieces and simmer them in the sauce for 15 minutes. Add the water, bring it to a boil, cover the pan, and cook for 20 minutes. When the red of the paprika rises to the surface (the red cheeks), the chicken should be tender. Serve warm with rice and *naan*.

Serves 6.

ANGHARE KEBAB
Charcoal-Barbecued Chicken Legs

This is a specialty of Kashmir and a good way to prepare chicken legs. I always cut a one-inch gash in the thick part of the legs since it opens them up to both the marinade and later to the cooking heat.

10 cloves garlic, crushed fine
2 inches fresh ginger, crushed fine
10 dried hot red chilis, soaked in 1 cup water for 1 hour and ground to a paste
1 tablespoon ground fenugreek (see Glossary), toasted lightly in a skillet
1 tablespoon ground cumin
1 tablespoon ground coriander
1 teaspoon turmeric
1 cup yoghurt
1 tablespoon fresh lemon juice
1 egg, beaten
1 tablespoon honey
Pinch ground saffron
12 chicken legs, with a 1-inch gash cut into the thick end of each

1. In a food processor process all the ingredients together, except the chicken legs, to a smooth paste. Marinate the legs in the mixture, covered, for 4–5 hours in the refrigerator.
2. Grill the legs, turning them, over charcoal for about 10 minutes. They may also be grilled under a gas or electric broiler, but over charcoal is more traditional and adds the flavor of smoke. Serve with mint sauce.

Serves 6.

BATAK CURRY
Duck Curry

It would seem inevitable that with seemingly tens of thousands of ducks paddling around the lakes of Kashmir traditional cooks would create a spicy and magical curry. And they have.

A 4 1/2- to 5-pound duck, loose skin and all fat removed
4 cloves garlic, sliced
1 1/2 inch fresh ginger, sliced
2 medium onions, sliced (1 cup)
1/2 cup yoghurt
1 teaspoon turmeric
1 tablespoon ground coriander
1 tablespoon ground cumin
1 teaspoon salt, or to taste
1 teaspoon paprika
1 teaspoon hot red chili powder
1 cup chopped fresh tomato
3 tablespoons corn oil
4 cups water
3 tablespoons chopped fresh coriander (Chinese parsley)

1. Rinse the duck well in cold water and cut into 10 pieces. Set aside.
2. Prepare the paste: In a food processor process together the garlic, ginger, onions, yoghurt, turmeric, coriander, cumin, salt, paprika, chili powder, and tomato to a smooth paste.
3. Heat the oil in a pan, add the spice paste, and cook over low heat for 5 minutes to integrate the flavors.
4. Add the duck pieces and stir-fry over low heat for 5 minutes. Add the water, bring to a boil, cover the pan, and simmer over low heat until the duck is tender, about 45 minutes to 1 hour. (You may have to extend the cooking time, depending upon the tenderness of the duck.) Garnish with the fresh coriander. Serve warm with rice and *naan*.

Serves 6 or 7.

BATAK BHUNA
Stuffed Duck Roast

The lakes in the Vale of Kashmir are filled with flocks of ducks swimming here and there. They dodge the canoes that ply the waters, their owners doing errands that take them from shore to houseboat to the island mosque. Ducks are everywhere. They are valued for their meat as well as for their eggs.

This popular duck roast is essentially for the tables of the upper classes in Kashmir. It is elegant, filled with the flavor of the ducks that have been feeding on the natural greens of the lakes.

THE STUFFING

    1 cup dried mixed fruit, such as apricots, prunes, and apples, halved
    2 tablespoons chopped fresh mint
  1/4 cup basmati rice, well rinsed, soaked in water 1 hour and drained
1 1/2 teaspoons black or white salt
    4 whole cloves
    1 teaspoon cuminseed
    1 duck liver, cut into 1/2-inch cubes
     A 4 1/2- to 5-pound duck, well cleaned and loose skin and all fat removed

THE SAUCE

 10 cups water
  2 medium onions, chopped (1 cup)
  5 cloves garlic, chopped
1 1/2 inches fresh ginger, chopped
  1 teaspoon salt, or to taste

1. Prepare the stuffing: Mix all the stuffing ingredients together well. Stuff the cavity of the duck and sew it up with a needle and thread. Set aside.
2. Prepare the sauce: Put the water, onions, garlic, ginger, salt, and the stuffed duck in a large pan. Bring to a boil, cover the pan, and cook over low heat for 45 minutes, turning the duck over once during this time. This should be enough time to ten-

derize the duck. Remove and set aside. Continue to simmer the sauce until it has been reduced to 2 cups.

3. Put the duck in a roasting pan and pour the sauce over it. Bake in a preheated 350 degree oven for about 20 minutes, basting occasionally, until the duck is brown.

Remove the duck from the oven and cut it into 10 pieces. Serve warm with the stuffing and sauce. Customarily, *Subje* (page 274) is served with this duck.

Serves 10 with bread, rice, and other dishes.

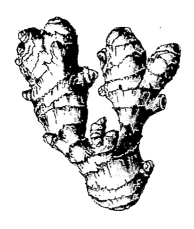

TITR KA ACHAR
Partridges Braised in Spiced Cream Sauce

This is a royal recipe of the Moghul era with a multitude of spices, seasonings, and flavors to match. The wild partridge, tender and flavored with the natural foods of the countryside, were shot or captured in nets by the thousands and served up in this delectable sauce.

   3 *tablespoons mustard oil*
   1 *cup chopped onion*
   6 *cloves garlic, chopped fine*
   1 *tablespoon chopped fresh ginger*
1/4 *cup yoghurt*
   1 *teaspoon turmeric*
   1 *teaspoon paprika*
1/2 *cup milk*
1/2 *cup heavy cream*
   1 *green mango, peeled, sliced, and grated or chopped fine*
   1 *cup chopped ripe tomato*
1/2 *teaspoon* garam masala *(see Glossary)*
   6 *partridges, cleaned (about 6 pounds in all)*

1. Heat the mustard oil in a skillet and over moderate/low heat brown the onion, garlic, and ginger for 2 minutes. Remove the solids with a slotted spoon and mix them briskly into the yoghurt. Add the turmeric and paprika and stir to combine. Set aside.
2. Mix the milk, cream, and mango together. Set aside.
3. Combine the yoghurt mixture with the mustard oil from the skillet, the milk/cream mixture, the tomato, and *garam masala*. Simmer the spiced mixture over low heat until the oil rises, about 5 minutes. Add the partridges, cover the pan, and simmer for 15–20 minutes, basting occasionally. Test the birds for tenderness; if still too firm cook until soft. Serve the partridges and sauce warm with bread and pilau.

Serves 6.

NOTE: This dish may be stored, covered, in the refrigerator for up to 1 week. When ready to serve, rewarm briefly. I have also used the same recipe with halved Cornish hens to good advantage. The cooking time should be extended to 1/2 hour or slightly more even.

Quail may also be used, but as they are smaller than partridge allow 2 or possibly 3 quail per person.

BADAMI KOFTA
Almond Balls in Creamy Tomato Sauce

This is a Kashmiri Brahman Hindu vegetarian dish prepared for special occasions. I often consider the origin of the ingredients in a recipe and realize that originally the cottage cheese, yoghurt, and tomato sauce were all homemade. Garlic, ginger, and onions were reduced to a smooth purée on a rectangular stone platform with a handheld stone cylinder that pushed the spices and other ingredients back and forth. Now we use a food processor but I doubt that anything is lost in the transition.

1/2 pound white or yellow pumpkin, peeled and grated
1 pound potatoes (4), boiled in their skins, peeled, and grated
1/2 cup cottage cheese, squeezed through a kitchen towel
1 tablespoon chopped fresh coriander (Chinese parsley)
1 cup blanched almonds, 12 reserved for stuffing
1 cup moistened, softened white bread, squeezed dry
1 cup corn oil for frying
1 cup milk
1 cup yoghurt
1 cup canned tomato sauce
4 cloves garlic and 1 inch fresh ginger, ground together to a paste
1 teaspoon paprika
1 teaspoon salt, or to taste

1. In a food processor process the pumpkin, potatoes, cheese, coriander, almonds, bread, and salt to a firm dough. Shape the dough into 12 balls and stuff each ball with 1 whole almond.
2. Heat the oil until hot in a wok and deep-fry the balls, a few at a time, over moderate/low heat until brown, about 3 minutes. Drain on paper towels.
3. Prepare the sauce: Put the milk, yoghurt, tomato sauce, ginger/garlic paste, paprika, salt, and 2 tablespoons oil, removed from the wok, in a large pan. Simmer over low heat for 15 min-

utes, add the balls, and cook 10 minutes more. Serve warm with rice and bread.

Serves 6.

NOTE: Almond balls can be served as a snack without the sauce. Prepare them up to Step 2 and serve them warm with a mint dipping sauce.

SAFFRANI CHAWAL
Saffron Rice

Saffron is the most expensive seasoning—it cannot be considered a spice—in the culinary firmament. It is the dried stigma plucked from the flower of the crocus (*Crocus sativus*). It is no wonder that the enormous expense has elevated saffron to astronomical heights. A pinch or two here and there is all that is generally used, but where saffron is easily available and reasonably priced, such as in Turkey and North Africa, a large quantity is more potent.

I have seen the hills in Kashmir covered with the flowering crocus plants waiting to be harvested. But beware! A Persian cook told me that too much saffron in the food will bring on bouts of hysterical laughter.

    3 tablespoons corn oil
    1 medium onion, chopped fine (1/2 cup)
 1/2 inch cinnamon stick
    3 bay leaves
    4 whole cloves
    4 green cardamom pods
    1 teaspoon cuminseed
    2 cloves garlic, crushed to a paste
 1/2 inch fresh ginger, crushed to a paste
    3 cups warm water
 1/2 cup yoghurt
 1/4 cup chopped fresh tomato
 1/2 teaspoon saffron
    6 dried pitted prunes
    6 dried apricots
    1 pound (2 cups) basmati rice, well rinsed, soaked in water 1/2 hour and drained

1. Heat the oil in a large ovenproof pan until hot, add the onion, and stir-fry it over low heat until light brown. Add the cinnamon stick, bay leaves, cloves, cardamom pods, cuminseed, and garlic and ginger pastes. Cook for 5 minutes.
2. Add the water, yoghurt, tomato, saffron, prunes, and apricots.

Bring the mixture to a boil and add the rice, mixing well. When the rice has absorbed the liquid, cover the pan with a clean, damp cloth and the pan cover. Place the pan in a preheated 350 degree oven and bake the rice for 7 minutes. The rice may be kept warm: Turn off the oven and let the pan stand in the oven until ready to serve.

Serve with Chaplee Kebab (page 256)—or any kind of kebab or curry.

Serves 6.

SUBJE
Vegetarian Side Dish

This side dish is a suggested (also traditional) accompaniment to *Batak Bhuna* (page 265). In addition, it also fulfills the vegetarian's search for Asian food that can replace meat, poultry, eggs, and seafood. The mark of good vegetarian food is that upon finishing eating it you have not noticed the absence of meat. This *subje* is not only traditional, but delicious and all-encompassing as well.

1 pound cauliflower, cut into 1-inch cubes
1 carrot, cut into 2-inch julienne (1 cup)
1 potato, peeled and cut into 1/2-inch cubes (1 cup)
1 cup string beans, cut into 2-inch lengths
1 cup fresh green peas
1 teaspoon salt, or to taste
1 1/2 teaspoons turmeric
3 cups water
2 cups yoghurt
1 cup chopped fresh tomato
3 tablespoons corn oil
6 cloves garlic, chopped
1 1/2 teaspoons cuminseed
5 whole dried hot red chilis
1 teaspoon paprika
2 tablespoons chopped fresh coriander (Chinese parsley) for garnish

1. Put the cauliflower, carrot, potato, beans, peas, salt, 1/2 teaspoon of the turmeric, and water in a pan. Bring to a boil and cook over moderate heat for 5 minutes. Drain.
2. Prepare the sauce: Mix the yoghurt and tomato together. Put the oil in a large pan and add the garlic, cuminseed, chilis, the remaining 1 teaspoon turmeric, and paprika and sauté over low heat for 5 minutes. Add the yoghurt/tomato mixture and mix well.
3. Add all the vegetables and cook, covered, over low heat for 15 minutes. Garnish with the coriander. Serve warm.

Serves 6 or more.

SUBJE KEBAB
Vegetable Barbecue

During the Golden Era, at the time of the Aryans in ancient India, King Vikrama Ditta devised this barbecue, one of his favorite vegetarian foods. It is an old, authentic recipe that is just as valid and popular now as it was then. Vegetarianism, by the way, is an ancient proclivity of the Hindus, not a contemporary discovery to fulfill the new emphasis on the abstinence from meat, eggs, and fish in one's diet.

It should be pointed out that not all the ingredients in this dish are of Asian origin. Cauliflower, an import from Europe, was brought there by the English colonials, whereas the potato's botanical origin is South and Central America via the Spanish to Europe and thence to Asia. Both vegetables were immediately welcomed into the mainstream of Indian cooking.

There are no eggs or oil in the vegetable mixture. Also, there is a long list of ingredients that produces many subtle flavors and could only be adhered to in an era, and a royal one at that, when there were many servants to work in the kitchen.

1 green banana, peeled, boiled in water to soften but still firm, and chopped
1 medium potato (4 ounces) peeled, boiled in water to soften but still firm, and chopped
1 carrot (2 ounces) boiled in water to soften but still firm and chopped
1/2 pound fresh spinach, leaves only, chopped fine
6 florets cauliflower (3 ounces), chopped fine
1 teaspoon pomegranate concentrate (available in Middle Eastern markets)
1 teaspoon ground cumin
1/4 teaspoon garam masala
1 small hot green chili, chopped fine (1–2 teaspoons)
1 scallion, chopped fine
2 cloves garlic, chopped fine
1 teaspoon finely chopped ginger
1 tablespoon chopped fresh coriander (Chinese parsley)
2 tablespoons chick-pea flour (besan)
2 tablespoons dry bread crumbs
1 teaspoon salt, or to taste
3 tablespoons corn oil

1. Mix all the ingredients together, except the oil, toss well, then roll into a sort of dough. (The *besan*, bread crumbs, and the natural moisture of the vegetables will hold it all together.) Form the dough mixture into 12 balls, each 1 1/2 inches in diameter, and divide them among several metal skewers, pushing them on.
2. Grill the skewers over charcoal or under a gas or electric broiler until brown. Or, the kebabs may be pan-fried in corn oil over moderate heat until brown on all sides. Drain on paper towels.

Serves 6.

ALOO AUR PHAY
Lotus and Potato Curry

Thin slices of lake lotus here show off their interior cut-out design, retain their characteristic crunch, and contrast well with the softer texture of potato cubes. All is seasoned Kashmiri style, meaning one texture is artfully played against another.

3 tablespoons corn oil
4 clove garlic, chopped
1 inch fresh ginger, chopped
1 tablespoon coriander seed
1 tablespoon cuminseed
1/2 teaspoon turmeric
1 teaspoon hot red chili powder
1 teaspoon salt, or to taste
1/2 cup yoghurt
1/2 cup chopped fresh tomato
1 1/2 cups water
1 pound lotus, sliced thin (2 cups), cooked in boiling water for 10 minutes and drained
1 1/2 pounds potatoes, peeled and cut into 1/2-inch cubes
1 tablespoon chopped fresh coriander (Chinese parsley)

1. Heat the oil in a pan, add the garlic, ginger, coriander seed, cuminseed, turmeric, chili powder, and salt and stir-fry over low heat for 5 minutes.
2. Add the yoghurt, tomato, and water and bring to a boil. Add the cooked lotus and the uncooked potatoes and simmer for 15 minutes. Serve warm garnished with the coriander. Serve with rice and *chapatti*.

Serves 6.

GUCHI MATTAR
Wild Mushrooms and Peas

Kashmir is a home for the wild morel mushroom, which is known there as *guchi*. It has a distinctive shape, with crisscross ridges around the gnome-like cap. Kashmiris collect fresh *guchi* during the rainy spring season and use them fresh, or they dry them for future use, including commerce. I spent a lot of time in Kashmir and never left without a bag of dried *guchi*, which one can buy at an exorbitant price in the bazaar most of the year. Dried *guchi* should be covered in water overnight, which reconstitutes their shape; drain before using.

1 cup chopped onion
1/2 inch fresh ginger, chopped
4 cloves garlic, chopped
1 teaspoon turmeric
1 teaspoon hot red chili powder
1 teaspoon salt, or to taste
1 cup water
3 tablespoons corn oil
1 teaspoon cuminseed
1 cup (about 25 grams) dried guchi (dried morels), soaked in water overnight, drained, and halved or quartered
1 cup fresh green peas
1/2 cup yoghurt
1 cup chopped fresh tomato
1 tablespoon chopped fresh coriander

1. In a food processor grind together the onion, ginger, garlic, turmeric, chili powder, and salt with 2 tablespoons of the water to moisten the mixture.
2. Put the oil in a pan, add the cuminseed, and stir-fry it over low heat for 10 seconds. Add the spice paste and stir-fry for 5 minutes. Add the *guchi*, peas, yoghurt, and tomato and stir-fry for 5 minutes. Add the remaining water, bring to a boil, and simmer, uncovered, for 10 minutes. Serve warm garnished with the coriander and with *chapatti* or other Indian breads.

Serves 6.

Dried Chinese black mushrooms are a substitute for dried *guchi*, although they do not have the same taste. (It is close enough, however.) Soak the mushrooms in water for 2 hours, drain, and halve.

Another variation includes potato with *guchi*. Peel 4 small potatoes (3/4 pound) and quarter them. Use the same list of ingredients as above but eliminate the peas. Cook 10 minutes longer to soften the potatoes.

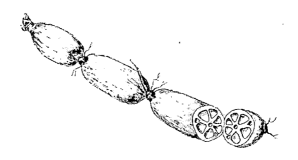

PUDEENA CHUTNEY
Mint and Coriander Chutney

The aromatic combination of fresh mint and coriander leaves produces a chutney for all seasons and culinary situations. For a more intense flavor, I sometimes omit the yoghurt, which has its own unique character but dilutes the strength of the herbs.

2 cups fresh mint leaves, stems removed
1 cup fresh coriander (Chinese parsley) leaves
1 small onion, chopped fine (1/4 cup)
1 hot green chili, chopped fine
1 cup yoghurt
1 tablespoon fresh lemon juice
4 scallions, sliced
1 green mango, peeled and the pulp chopped fine (optional)
1/2 teaspoon salt
1 teaspoon cuminseed, toasted

In a food processor process all the ingredients until smooth. Serve with Grilled Breast of Chicken Chop (page 261) or any other frontier-cooking meat dish.

Makes about 1 1/2 cups.

CHAT MASALA
A Spicy Food-Enhancer

Chat masala is a spice/seasoning that enhances the flavors of food. Some Asian cuisines use the chemical MSG to do the same thing, but *chat masala* is a natural combination that does add flavor and promotes good taste.

2 *tablespoons black or regular salt*
1 *tablespoon ground cumin*
1 *teaspoon black pepper*
1 *teaspoon sour salt*
1 *teaspoon* ajowan *(see Glossary) seed*
1/8 *teaspoon* hing *(asafoetida, see Glossary)*

Mix all the ingredients together. Store in a jar with a tight cover.

Makes about 1/4 cup.

GARAM MASALA
Hot Spice Mixture

There are as many recipes and personal preferences for *garam masala* as there are cooks in the frontier provinces. This particular mixture is from the traditional memory of Panna Lal Sharma and is inspired by the palates of Afghanistan and Pakistan.

2 *tablespoons cuminseed*
2 *tablespoons coriander seed*
1 *inch cinnamon stick*
5 *whole cloves*
1 *tablespoon black peppercorns*
4 *bay leaves*
5 *green cardamom pods*
4 *black cardamom pods (optional)*
1 *teaspoon fennel seed*
  Pinch ground nutmeg
  Pinch ground mace

1. Toast all the ingredients in a dry skillet over low heat for 5 minutes. (The aroma will rise during the toasting.) Cool.
2. Using a food processor, grind the spice mixture to a fine powder. Store in a jar with a tight cover.

Makes about 1/4 cup.

S O O J E E   K A
K H D A Z H A
Semolina Sweet (Halwa)

This is a wonderful Asian sweet, one of my favorites, which we know as cream of wheat. Semolina is the heart of the wheat kernel and is used to make bread, among other creations. The Burmese make a *soojee* cake that is covered with toasted poppy seeds. Everyone likes *soojee*.

Kashmiris say that semolina *halwa* is good for reviving flagging energy and thereby assign a medicinal value to what is an exceptional sweet. It is also told that the Moghul Emperor Shah Jehan of Taj Mahal fame and his beloved wife, Mumtaz (they produced thirteen children) adored *soojee*.

1 1/2 cups water
1/4 cup milk
1/4 cup sugar, or more to taste
5 cardamom pods, seeds only
   Pinch ground saffron
4 tablespoons butter or ghee (clarified butter)
1 cup semolina
2 tablespoons blanched almonds, chopped
10 unsalted cashew nuts, roasted
1 tablespoon golden or dark raisins
10 pistachio nuts, shelled

1. In a pan mix together the water, milk, sugar, cardamom seeds, and saffron and bring to a boil. Simmer, covered, over low heat for 10 minutes. Set aside.
2. Heat the butter in another pan, add the semolina, and toast it lightly over low heat until the aroma arises.
3. Slowly add the sugar/milk liquid, stirring continuously, for 5 minutes as the grain absorbs the liquid. Cover the pan and let stand for 5 minutes more.
4. Remove the *soojee* to a serving bowl and garnish with the almonds, cashews, raisins, and pistachio nuts. Always serve warm.

Serves 6.

LOKI KA HALWA (DOODHI)
White Pumpkin Sweet

> You can encounter the white pumpkin, also known as winter melon (*Ben-incasa hispida*), in New York City's Chinatown for many months of the year. When mature, the pumpkin is covered with a kind of white dust and is recognizable on account of it. Vegetable merchants cut this very large pumpkin in lengthwise slices and sell it piece by piece. In Calcutta, my cook used to cut the pumpkin into one-inch cubes and preserve it in sugar syrup.
>
> This sweet is soft in texture, light and sweet, and easy on the palate.

4 *pounds* loki *(white pumpkin, also known as winter melon)*
4 *cups milk*
1 *tablespoon butter or* ghee *(clarified butter)*
4 *tablespoons sugar*
  Pinch ground saffron
2 *tablespoons blanched almonds, chopped fine*
2 *tablespoons pistachio nuts, chopped fine*
1 *tablespoon raisins*
10 *cardamom pods, seeds only, crushed*

1. Peel the heavy outer skin from the *loki* and grate the pulp.
2. Bring the milk to a boil and simmer over low heat until reduced to 2 cups.
3. Put the butter and grated *loki* in a pan and sauté it over low heat for 5 minutes. Add the sugar, saffron, the reduced milk, half of the almonds and pistachios, the raisins, and crushed cardamom seeds. Combine well and simmer over low heat until very thick, about 20 minutes.

    Serve warm or cold on plates. Garnish each serving with the remaining almonds and pistachios.

Serves 6.

PHAL KA NASHA
Strawberry Yoghurt Frappé

Kashmir is famous in India for its wonderfully sweet and fragrant fruit, especially strawberries, which are picked ripe and immediately consumed. Prepared when the berries are fresh and sweet, this frappé is a typical hot-weather drink. During siesta time, when one wants to doze or relax, the frappé is a welcome aperitif, providing comfort, good taste, and the illusion of cool mountain air as in the Vale of Kashmir blowing over Dal Lake. For a while I lived on a houseboat and partook of all the romantic notions of the early Moghul emperors who sipped their *phal ka nasha* in the Shalimar Gardens.

2 *cups hulled fresh ripe strawberries, chopped coarse if large*
2 *cups yoghurt*
1 *tablespoon sugar, or to taste*
1 *tablespoon fresh mint leaves*
   Cracked ice cubes

In a food processor process everything together, except the ice cubes, to a smooth purée. Half-fill glasses with the ice and pour the strawberry mixture over it. Serve cold. May be eaten with a spoon.

Serves 6.

ANAR KA RUSS
Pomegranate Summer Drink

The pomegranate was known as the "apple of Carthage," which, perhaps, reveals its origin and certainly its popularity. Known in ancient times in the frontier regions of Afghanistan, Pakistan, and Kashmir, the pomegranate is especially admired in this summer drink. The soft white seeds that are surrounded by the acid pulp are processed and crushed so that they, too, become part of the drink.

4 *large ripe pomegranates, all seeds removed, husks discarded*
1 *cup milk*
  Pinch ground saffron
2 *tablespoons sugar*
  Ice cubes cracked and melted until slushy

In a food processor process the pomegranate seeds first for 1 minute to break them down and release their liquid. Then add the pulp, milk, saffron, and sugar and process until combined. Divide the ice among tall glasses and pour the pomegranate mixture over it. Stir each drink and serve immediately.

Serves 4 or 5.

MANGO KA LASSI
Mango-Flavored Yoghurt Punch

Mango, especially the Langra and Alfonso varieties, is the most popular of all fruit in all the regions of India. When it becomes available in New York City, I frequent any number of green markets to find the most fragrant. A good nose helps to make a good shopper. Yoghurt is frequently beaten into punch in India and Kashmir and when flavored with ripe mango in season is addictive.

1 large fresh ripe mango, peeled and sliced
4 cups yoghurt
2 tablespoons sugar, or to taste
1/2 cup milk
1 cup cracked ice cubes

In a food processor process the mango, yoghurt, sugar, and milk together until smooth. Strain through a metal sieve into a pitcher to remove any mango fibres. Add ice to tall glasses and pour in the mango punch. Serve cold.

Serves 4 or 5.

KASHMIRI KAVA
Kashmiri Tea

In a country where there is a huge population and very few modern medical facilities, the average man has depended on herbal medicines for centuries. My own inclination is to trust the native when he suggests an herb or concoction that will cure a malady. Kashmiri *kava* is an Ayurvedic medicinal tea and is included here for its taste as well as its historical purposes. Unsweetened, it is used as an antidote for diabetics. Green tea is also thought to prevent cancer of the esophagus (although this was not known to the Kashmiris).

Kava is imbibed during the cold weather to ward off the chills of winter. It is also served after dinner as a digestive that cleans the palate.

I am always astonished at the lengths the Indian preoccupation with spices and seasonings will go to create an ambiance that may or may not arrive at a culinary or medicinal destination. This tea includes the skin of arrowroot (*Maranta arundinacea*), which contains starch, and in the original recipe the miniature orchid-like flowers of the cardamom plant. Fennel leaves and green tea are the other unconventional ingredients. When tasting *kava* in Kashmir, I found it a bit too exotic for my taste, but nevertheless not unpleasant.

4 *cups water*
1 *tablespoon green leaf tea*
1 *inch fennel leaf, fresh or dried*
  Pinch ground saffron
4 *cardamom pods*
1 *teaspoon chopped fresh skin of arrowroot*
  Honey to taste

Bring the water to a boil. Add all the ingredients, except the honey, and simmer over low heat for 10 minutes. Serve hot or cool, with honey to taste.

Serves 6.

AN AFTERWORD

THE MIZOS—THE LOST TRIBE OF MANASSEH

Some time ago now, during my residence and various trips to Calcutta, there was a rumor floating about that a "Jewish sect" was to be found in the extreme east of India, near the Burmese border, either in the states of Manipur or Mizoram. I made several tentative inquiries but nothing of substance turned up to confirm the story.

However, on February 20, 1987, an exciting event occurred. *The New York Times* reported that, indeed, a group of Jews did exist who considered themselves to be the descendants of the tribe of Manasseh who were dispersed to other places at the time of the destruction of the Temple in Jerusalem in A.D. 72.

The Manasseh Jews, as they are known, also indicated that they were probably the same group that came to Asia as the Kaifeng, China, now-extinct community of Jews. There are many interpretations of the Mizos and their origin, but most are pure speculation, compounded by the lack of documentary evidence. The Mizos have not been discouraged by this and are forging ahead to press their claim to Judaism in Israel and India.

Most of the speculation came via the route of Christianity, since 90 percent of the people of the state of Mizoram are Christian, having been converted by Presbyterian missionaries at the end of the nineteenth century. Before that the tribal peoples of that hilly region were animists, believing in God and fearing the Devil.

But upon reflection the Mizos equated their own word-of-mouth ideas with what Christianity had taught them. There were so many coincidences between their origin and the ancient Jews and their dispersion from the Middle East that could not be refuted. So they claimed to be the Lost Tribe of Manasseh.

During November, 1994, while I was researching this book in Calcutta, I made a telephone call to Aizawl, the capital of Mizoram, in search of the leader of the Jewish community whose name was known to me. The difficulties were frustrating; telephone lines were cut, or upon reaching the family, indistinct. This sort of thing went on for several weeks, when at last I encouraged the leader to send several persons who knew the cuisine and could describe their food. Since no foreigner is allowed into this politically fragile region, I promised to pay for their air transport to and from Aizawl. Even this was fraught with danger since roads were blocked by insurgents.

Ultimately, surprisingly, and without warning, two young, attractive people, a married couple with Oriental features of the hill regions, arrived at my hotel and work began.

Random notes about their eating habits as reported to me revealed the strangeness of the Mizo way of life in earlier days, and now. The Mizos were known as, "the people of the hills" who lived in agricultural communities. Most people have small vegetable plots. They are rice-eaters as are the other people of India. Meat is an essential ingredient of their diet. They are big meat-eaters, predominantly pork, except for the Jews who maintain kashrut to the best of their ability. Both the Christian and Jewish communities eat the same foods, with the exception of pork. Pork is the cheapest meat followed by beef, with chicken being the most expensive.

For the most part, firewood is used for cooking but gas cylinders are also available and are used depending upon who can afford them. Since dried vegetables are used during the winter months, when fresh items are not available, there is a rack in the kitchen above the heating unit. Vegetables are placed on the rack and dried as long as necessary to preserve them.

Of special interest are the popular sweet potatoes and their leaves. The young, tender leaves are eaten fresh. The large leaves are dried in the sun for ten to fifteen days. In a peculiar system, the stems of the leaf are broken every inch to dry faster while the entire leaf is hung over bamboo rods. After drying, the leaves are tied in round bundles and dried further on a platform near the wood fire where the smoke is said to improve the flavor. In the winter months the bundles are soaked in water, quartered, then dropped into boiling water with hot chili and salt, and cooked for 15 minutes. One bundle serves five people.

We are dealing here with the simplest of foods contrived by mountain and jungle people.

The following is the general eating routine of the Mizos:

Early morning tea. Black tea is the beverage of choice. No breakfast.
Lunch is eaten at 8 A.M.
Noon is snack time.
School is out at 4 P.M. (The Mizos have one of the highest literacy rates in all of India.) Businesses close at 5 P.M. Dinner is eaten from 5 to 6 P.M. Tea without sugar is taken after each meal.

Now, many families have gone to Israel attempting to be identified with the Judaic way of life. The road is difficult because in order to be included the Mizos must have sufficient proof of their antecedents.

But the Mizos are not discouraged.

HOLIDAY COOKING

The following letter was sent to me by messenger in Calcutta during the time when I was attempting to find Mizo cooks from the Jewish community. I am including this as it was written since it contains all the information as expressed by the writer, Chazan Gideon Rei, the leader of the community.

Dear Mr. Copeland.
If you want to include these few lines of the method of cooking our food for holiday use as the following:
The sevet Manashe use to prepare a special dine for Sabbath and holidays. That the most importance item is Baker loaf or bread which mixed by a small quantity of sugar on Sabbath and holidays for the use of Kiddush which baking by ourselves and bakery shops.
Chicken curry is the most prevailing customary on Jewish auspicious days. After removed the blood by: (a) soaking (b) salting (c) Rinsing as per Jewish law, the meat is set down on a diagonal slant position apropriet for the salting stage.
And the concoction of chicken or animal is generally—there are three kinds of method viz.—(a) Frying with some spices

and turmeric. Sometime we add a small quantity of water (b) Hotch potch of meat and rice with added some garlics, gingers and good odour of herbs. (c) Cooking meat by boiling it with a lot of water (Undiluted by water) such as for soup.

On specific holidays such as Purim, Chanukkah and Shimchat Torah, we use to set the social banquet. We slaughter Ox, Sheep, He-goat or sometime also the Fish.

These permited animals we eat after preparing through the laws of Kashrut. Generally, beef is concocted simply by cooking with a lot of water for the feast. Sometime, meat is fry with ingredient of some species, garlicsw and gingers ek.t.c. The slaughter of aminals have done just a day of before holiday.

On Shavuoth. We use to eat a lot of dairy food, cheese making from milk.

On Purim, we eat a kind of flat loaf which has three corners.

On Pe(s)ach, we bake a flour of wheat without mixtur of any kind of species as for Matzoth. This local made Matzah is very difficult to consume because of no expert to bake it.

YOUR'S

(GIDEON REI)

A R S A K A N
Chicken Curry, Mizo Style

Meat is money, and while a chicken is expensive, it can feed many. This curry is prepared to serve ten, with substantial sauce, along with a large portion of rice. Cardamom, which grows in Mizoram, is frequently included in their cooking. Oil is liked there and is added in quantity. As prepared here, this is an economical dish.

1/2 cup mustard oil
2 medium onions, sliced (1 cup)
4 cloves garlic, crushed to a paste
2 inches fresh ginger, crushed to a paste
2 ripe tomatoes (1/2 pound), sliced
1 teaspoon salt, or to taste (Mizos like salt and use it liberally)
1 teaspoon garam masala (see Glossary)
2 whole cardamom pods
1 chicken (3 pounds), cut into 10 pieces
2 cups water

1. Heat the oil in a pan over moderate heat. Add the onions and stir-fry for 1 minute. Add the garlic, ginger, tomatoes, salt, garam masala, and cardamom pods and stir rapidly.
2. Add the chicken pieces and stir-fry them for 10 minutes until brown. Add the water, cover the pan, and simmer over low heat for 1/2 hour. There should be substantial sauce. Serve warm with plenty of cooked rice.

Serves 10.

CRAB AND SESAME
SEED CHUTNEY

This recipe is included for historical purposes only since from the *kashrut* point of view, crabs are not a kosher food but are, nevertheless, eaten by the Jewish Mizos.

Small freshwater crabs are found in the Mizoram rivers. They are prepared in this chutney in small quantities and are considered to be an expensive dish.

25 *live small river crabs*
1/2 *pound sesame seeds*
1 *tablespoon salt*

1. Drop the crabs into boiling water to kill them. (This also cleans them.) Drain.
2. Crush the crabs, a few at a time, in a mortar and pestle of wood, stone, or metal, but wood is preferred. Separately, crush the sesame seeds. Then mix the crab, sesame seeds, and salt together and put the mixture in a pan. Cover with a leaf, such as a banana leaf. Place the pan near the wood fire or other warm place in the kitchen, for 4 to 5 days. Do not place on the fire.
3. To use, take a small amount, about 1 tablespoon for each person, and stir-fry it lightly in 1 teaspoon vegetable oil for 1 minute. Add 1 tablespoon chopped onion to the stir-fry. Eat with the meal.

   To preserve the chutney that remains, stir-fry all of it in oil with chopped onion. Set aside for other meals.

Makes about one cup.

✄ INDEX ✄

stew, baby goat shank, 250
strawberry yoghurt frappé, 284
stuffed:
  bean curd, 32
  cabbage rolls, 113–14
  duck roast, 265–66
  eggplant or zucchini squash, 115
  grape leaves, 110–11
  mango pickle, 97
  okra, tamarind-, 61
  packets, miniature, 117–18
  steamed dumplings Bhutan style,
    168–69
  vegetables, 112
sweet-and-sour prawns, 27–28
sweets, *see* desserts and sweets
Swiss chard:
  pork and, 207
  soup with pork, 203

tamarind:
  fish in a *kerai*, 239
  -stuffed okra, 61
tea:
  Bhutanese butter, 192
  Kashmiri, 289
  spiced, 72–73
tofu, *see* bean curd
tomato(es):
  Armenian meat patties, 128
  bean curd with black mushrooms
    and, 31
  cauliflower, and potato stir fry,
    47–48
  chutney, 84
  chutney, cooked, 220
  ground beef fry, 208
  kasundi, 85
  kasundi, a pickle, 103
  lamb and vegetable soup, 108
  and pork curry, 184
  rice, lamb, and vegetable pilau, 109
  sauce, creamy, almond balls in,
    269–70
  stuffed, 112
  table chutney, 219
tongue and brain combination, beef,
  175–76
tree ears, viii–ix, 224
  jungle, 224

vegetable(s):
  assorted, fried noodles with, 15
  barbecue, 274–75
  and beef cutlet, 122–23
  fresh assorted, pickle, 90
  and lamb soup, 108
  mixed, with chicken, 22
  rice, and lamb pilau, 109
  and shrimp curry, 150–51
  soup, Buddhist, 11
  stuffed, 112
  vegetarian side dish, 273
  see also specific vegetables
vegetarian dishes, 36–38, 274
  almond balls in creamy tomato
    sauce, 269–70
  bean curd with tomato and black
    mushrooms, 31
  Buddhist vegetable soup, 11
  cauliflower, potato, and tomato stir
    fry, 47–48
  cauliflower stir fry, 47
  chick-pea flour pancakes, 51
  chick-peas in an especially spiced
    sauce, 49–50
  Chinese white radish in black bean
    sauce, 33
  cucumber and capsicum mix, 56
  cucumber and lentil mix, 55
  cucumber salad in mustard sauce, 57
  cucumber-stuffed semolina
    pancakes, 58–59
  fried noodles with assorted
    vegetables, 15
  fried wontons with potato and
    cashew stuffing, 6
  ground millet gruel, 46
  lentil balls with yoghurt sauce,
    67–68
  long beans in yoghurt sauce, 64
  lotus and potato curry, 276
  mixed greens omelette, 121
  mushroom, cauliflower, and cashew
    stir fry, 34
  red spinach and spice, 63
  rice, spices, and water chestnuts,
    65–66
  sausages and rice, 54
  sausages in spiced yoghurt sauce,
    52–53